CONTENTS

PREFACE 3

Unit One – Art. 90 thru Art. 200 9

Unit Two – Art. 210 20

Unit Three – Art. 215 thru 240 31

Unit Four – Art. 250 42

Unit Five – Art. 300 thru 310 53

Unit Six – Art. 314 thru 332 64

Unit Seven – Art. 334 thru 356 75

Unit Eight – Art. 358 thru 388 87

Unit Nine – Art. 390 thru 406 99

Unit Ten – Art. 408 thru 426 110

Unit Eleven – Art. 430 thru 480 122

Unit Twelve – Art. 500 thru 516 134

Unit Thirteen – Art. 517 thru 550 146

Unit Fourteen – Art. 551 thru 630 157

Unit Fifteen – Art. 645 thru 680 169

Unit Sixteen – Art. 682 thru 725 181

Unit Seventeen – Art. 760 thru Appendix C 193

Unit Eighteen – FINAL EXAM #1 205

Unit Nineteen – FINAL EXAM #2 217

Unit Twenty – FINAL EXAM #3 229

Copyright 2016   BrownTechnical.org

Answer Key – Unit One 241

Answer Key – Unit Two 242

Answer Key – Unit Three 243

Answer Key – Unit Four 244

Answer Key – Unit Five 245

Answer Key – Unit Six 246

Answer Key – Unit Seven 247

Answer Key – Unit Eight 248

Answer Key – Unit Nine 249

Answer Key – Unit Ten 250

Answer Key – Unit Eleven 251

Answer Key – Unit Twelve 252

Answer Key – Unit Thirteen 253

Answer Key – Unit Fourteen 254

Answer Key – Unit Fifteen 255

Answer Key – Unit Sixteen 256

Answer Key – Unit Seventeen 257

Answer Key – Unit Eighteen – Final Exam #1 258

Answer Key – Unit Nineteen – Final Exam #2 259

Answer Key – Unit Twenty – Final Exam #3 260

PREFACE

HOW TO PREPARE FOR THE EXAM

This book is a guide to prepare for the electricians' exam and to review sections of the NEC® that the electrician may encounter during his/her day-to-day work experiences. It will not make you a competent electrician, nor teach you the electrical trade, but it will give you an idea of the type of questions asked on most electricians' examinations.

Most electrical exams consist of multiple-choice questions and this is the type of questions reflected in this textbook. These questions will give you a feel for how many of the examinations nationwide are structured. These questions are an example of the many questions the author has encountered when taking numerous exams in recent years.

Begin your pre-exam preparation with two points in mind.
* Opportunities in life will arise - be prepared for them.
* The more you LEARN - the more you EARN.

Attempting to take an exam without preparation is a complete waste of time. Attend classes at your local community college. Attend seminars, electrical code updates, and company sponsored programs. Many major electrical suppliers and local unions sponsor classes of this type at no cost. Take advantage of them.

Become familiar with the National Electrical Code®; the Code has a LANGUAGE all its own. Understanding the language will help one to better interpret the NEC® Do not become intimidated by its length. Become thoroughly familiar with the definitions in Chapter One, if you don't, the remainder of the NEC® will be difficult to comprehend. Remember, on the job we use different "lingo" and phrases compared to the way the NEC® is written and to the way many test questions are expressed.

HOW TO STUDY

Before beginning to study, get into the right frame of mind, be relaxed. Study in a quiet place that is conducive to learning. If such a place is not available, go to your local library. It is important that you have a quiet, relaxed atmosphere in which to study.

It is much better to study many short lengths of time than attempt to study fewer, longer lengths of time. Try to study a little while, say about an hour, every evening. You will need the support and understanding of your family to set aside this much needed time.

As you study this exam preparation book and other references, highlight important points with a highlighter. This makes it easier to locate Code references when taking the exam.

Copyright 2016

Use a straight edge, such as a six inch ruler when using the NEC® tables and charts. A very common mistake is to get on the wrong line when using these tables; if this happens, the result is an incorrect answer.

Use tabs on the major sections of your NEC®, this makes it easier and takes less time to locate these major sections when taking the exam. The national average allowed per question is three minutes, you cannot waste time.

WHAT TO STUDY
A common reason for one to be unsuccessful when attempting to pass the electricians' exam is not knowing what to study. Approximately forty percent of most exams are known as "core" questions. This type of question is asked on most exams, and is reflected in this exam preparation textbook.

The subject matter covered in most electrical license examinations is:

* Grounding and bonding
* Overcurrent protection
* Wiring methods and installation
* Boxes and fittings
* Services and equipment
* Motors
* Special occupancies
* Load calculations
* Lighting
* Appliances
* Box and raceway fill
* Hazardous locations

Become very familiar with questions on the above referenced subject matter. Knowing what to study is a major step to passing your exam.

HELPFUL HINTS ON TAKING THE EXAM

* <u>Complete the easy questions and "gimmies" first.</u> On most tests, all questions are valued the same. If you become too frustrated on any one question, it may reflect upon your entire test.

* <u>Keep track of time.</u> Do not spend too much time on one question. If a question is difficult for you, mark on the answer sheet the answer you think is correct and place a check (✓) by that question in the examination booklet. Then go on to the next question; if you have time after finishing the rest of the exam, you can go back to the questions you have checked. If you simply do not know the answer to a question, guess. Choose the answer that is most familiar to you. In most cases, the answer is B or C.

* <u>Only change answers if you know you are right.</u> - Usually, your first answer is your best answer.

* <u>Relax</u> - Do not get uptight and stressed out when testing.

* <u>Tab your Code Book.</u> - References are easier and faster to find.

* <u>Use a straightedge.</u> - Prevent getting on the wrong line when referring to the tables in the NEC®.

* <u>Get a good nights rest before the exam.</u> - Do not attempt to drive several hours to an exam site; be rested and alert.

* <u>Understand the question.</u> - One key word in a question can make a difference in what the question is asking. Underlining key words in the question will help you to understand the meaning of the question.

* <u>Use a dependable calculator.</u> - Use a solar powered calculator that has a battery back-up. Many test sites are not well lighted; this type of calculator will prepare you for such a situation. Perhaps, bring along a spare calculator.

* <u>Show up at least 30 minutes prior to your exam time.</u> - You may allow yourself even more time for traffic, etc.

TYPICAL REGULATIONS AT THE PLACE OF EXAMINATION

To ensure that all examinees are examined under equally favorable conditions, the following regulations and procedures are observed at most examination sites:

1. Each examinee must present proper photo identification, preferably his/her driver's license before he/she will be permitted to take the examination.

2. Each examinee is assigned to a seat specifically designated by name and/or number when admitted to the examination room.

3. No one will be permitted to work beyond the established time limits.

4. Examinees are not permitted any reference material EXCEPT the National Electrical Code®.

5. Examinees will be permitted to use noiseless calculators during the examination. Calculators which provide programmable ability or pre-programmed calculators are prohibited.

6. Permission of an examination proctor must be obtained before leaving the room while the examination is in progress.

TYPICAL EXAMINATION QUESTIONS

The examples on this page are intended to illustrate typical questions that may appear on electricians' exams.

EXAMPLE 1

An equipment grounding conductor of a branch circuit shall be identified by which of the following colors?

A. gray
B. white
C. black
D. green

Here you are asked to select from the listed colors the one that is to be used to identify the equipment grounding conductor of a branch circuit. Since Section 250.119 of the NEC® requires that green or green with yellow stripes be the color of insulation used on a grounding conductor (when it is not bare), the answer is **D**.

EXAMPLE 2

A circuit leading to a gasoline dispensing pump must have a disconnecting means:

A. only in the grounded conductors.
B. only in the ungrounded conductors.
C. operating independently in all conductors.
D. that simultaneously disconnects both the grounded and ungrounded conductors supplying the fuel dispensing pump.

Here the "question" is in the form of an incomplete statement. Your task is to select the choice that best completes the statement. In this case, you should have selected **D** since Section 514.11 of the NEC® specifies that such a circuit shall be provided with a means to disconnect simultaneously from the source of supply all conductors of a circuit, including the grounded conductor.

EXAMPLE 3

A building or other structure served shall be supplied by only one service EXCEPT one where the capacity requirements are in excess of _____.

A. 800 amperes at a supply voltage of 600 volts or less
B. 1000 amperes at a supply voltage of 600 volts or less
C. 1500 amperes at a supply voltage of 600 volts or less
D. 2000 amperes at a supply voltage of 600 volts or less

Again, the "question" is in the form of an incomplete statement and your task is to select the choice that best completes the statement. In this case, you are to find an exception. You have to select the condition that has to be met when supplying a building or structure by more than one service. You should have selected **D** because Section 230.2(C)(1) requires the conditions listed in **D** but does not require or permit the conditions listed in **A, B**, or **C**.

EXAMPLE 4

Disregarding exceptions, the MINIMUM size overhead service-drop conductors shall be _____ AWG copper.

A. 6
B. 8
C. 12
D. 14

Here the "question" is in the form of "fill in the blank" and your task is to select the choice that best completes the statement. In this case, exceptions are not applicable. You have to select the minimum size conductor required for overhead service-drop conductors. You should have selected **B** because Section 230.23(B) specifies that the conductors shall not be smaller than 8 AWG copper.

HOW TO USE THIS BOOK

Each "practice exam" or unit contained in this book consists of fifty questions. Since each unit, other than the "practice final exams", is identified as to the Article of the NEC® where questions are asked, it should take you no more than 90 minutes per unit to complete. Using this time limit as a standard, you should be able to complete an actual examination in the allotted time.

To get the most out of this book, you should answer every question and highlight your NEC® for future reference. If you have difficulty with a question, skip it and come back to it after completing the remainder of the questions. Review your answers with the **"ANSWER KEY"** at the back of this book. This will help you identify your strengths and weaknesses. When you discover you are weaker in some areas than others, you will know that further study is necessary in those areas.

Do only one or two "practice exams" contained in this book during an allotted study period; this way you do not get "burned out" and fatigued. This also helps you develop good study habits. **GOOD LUCK!**

ABOUT THE AUTHOR

H. Ray Holder has worked in the electrical industry for over fifty years as an apprentice, journeyman, master, field engineer, estimator, business manager, contractor, inspector, consultant, and instructor.

Mr. Holder is a graduate of Texas State University and holds a Bachelor of Science Degree in Occupational Education.

He is a certified instructor of electrical trades. His classes are presented in a simplified, easy-to-understand format for electricians.

He has taught thousands of students at Austin Community College and the University of Texas, at Austin, Texas, Odessa College, at Odessa, Texas, Technical-Vocational Institute of Albuquerque, New Mexico, and in the public school systems in Ft. Worth and San Antonio, Texas. He is currently the Director of Education for Electrical Seminars, Inc. of San Marcos, Texas.

Mr. Holder is an active member of the National Fire Protection Association, International Association of Electrical Inspectors, and retired member of the International Brotherhood of Electrical Workers.

OTHER TITLES AVAILABLE BASED ON THE 2011 NEC®

Electricians Practice Calculations Exams

Electricians Exam Book

Practical Calculations for Electricians

UNIT ONE

NEC® QUESTIONS FROM ARTICLE 90 THROUGH ARTICLE 200

The following National Electrical Code® questions are typical of questions encountered on all electricians' exams, based on the above referenced Articles of the Code. Select the best answer from the choices given then review your answers with the answer key at the back of this book.

ARTICLE 90 - INTRODUCTION
****

1. The National Electrical Code® is NOT:

A. designed for future expansion of electrical use.
B. designed to safeguard people and property from electrical hazards.
C. published by the NFPA.
D. intended as a specification manual for trained persons.

2. Which of the following locations are required to have electrical installations comply with the NEC®?

A. A luxury cruise ship
B. An underground mine
C. Marinas
D. Private use aircraft

3. The NEC® rules and provisions are enforced by:

A. the electrical utility company that provides the electrical power to the service.
B. the United States government.
C. the local authority having legal jurisdiction.
D. Underwriter Laboratories.

4. Formal interpretations of the NEC® may be found in the:

A. National Electrical Code® Handbook.
B. OSHA Standards.
C. Life and Safety Handbook.
D. NFPA Regulations Governing Committee Projects.

5. Which of the following listed is permitted to grant exception or amend the rules or mandate set forth by the NEC®?

A. architect
B. electrical engineer
C. job-site superintendent
D. authority having jurisdiction

6. Mandatory rules of the NEC® are those that identify actions that are specifically required or prohibited and are characterized by the use of the terms _____.

A. may or may not
B. can or cannot
C. will or will not
D. shall or shall not

ARTICLE 100 - DEFINITIONS
****

7. The ampacity of a conductor is defined by the NEC® to be the maximum current in amperes, a conductor can carry continuously under the conditions of use without exceeding _____.

A. its temperature rating
B. the allowable voltage drop limitations
C. its melting point
D. its rated voltage

8. An enclosure designed either for surface or flush mounting and provided with a frame in which a swinging door may be hung is a _____.

A. cabinet
B. cut-out box
C. panelboard
D. switchboard

9. A conductor whose purpose is to simply assure the required electrical continuity is a:

A. grounded conductor.
B. bonding conductor or jumper.
C. continuity conductor.
D. low impedance conductor.

10. The NEC® specifically defines the term "within sight" to be as close as practical to the equipment but, in no case more than how many feet?

A. 20 feet
B. 30 feet
C. 40 feet
D. 50 feet

11. Which of the following would be classified as a wet location?

   I. Conduit under a concrete slab in direct contact with the earth.
   II. Conduit above ground exposed to the weather.

A. I only
B. II only
C. both I and II
D. neither I nor II

12. A branch-circuit or feeder conductor that is intentionally grounded is a _____ conductor.

A. grounding
B. grounded
C. green colored
D. none of the above

13. Electrical wiring installed in an area located under an outdoor canopy or open porch, is said to be installed in a _____ location.

A. damp
B. dry
C. wet
D. hazardous

14. That portion of an electrical wiring system that is beyond the final overcurrent device protecting the circuit is known as the _____.

A. branch-circuit
B. feeder
C. sub-feeder
D. service-entrance conductors

15. The NEC® defines a "continuous load" to be a load where the maximum current is expected to continue for at LEAST _____ hours or more.

A. three
B. four
C. six
D. eight

16. A location that requires a ladder for access to an electrical wiring system or equipment but, does not require removal of the permanent structure is defined as being:

A. readily accessible.
B. semi-accessible.
C. non-accessible.
D. accessible.

17. Conductors from a switchboard feeding branch circuit overcurrent devices are defined as _____ conductors.

A. feeder
B. branch-circuit
C. service-entrance
D. service lateral

18. The underground conductors between the street main or from transformers, and the first point of connection to the service-entrance conductors in a meter are defined as the _____.

A. feeder conductors
B. service lateral
C. service-drop
D. branch-circuit conductors

19. A disconnect or main panel that is so constructed that exposure to a beating rain will not result in the entrance of water is defined as being _____.

A. watertight
B. rainproof
C. weatherproof
D. raintight

20. A point in the wiring system at which current is taken to supply utilization equipment such as luminaires and appliances is known as _____.

A. a receptacle
B. a junction box
C. an outlet
D. a service-entrance

21. The space under the raised floors of computer rooms where air ducts are connected and that forms part of the air distributions systems is know as a _____.

A. crawl space
B. air duct space
C. plenum
D. dedicated electrical space

22. A neutral conductor is always _____.

A. a grounded conductor
B. an ungrounded conductor
C. white in color
D. the conductor connected to the neutral point of a system that is intended to carry current under normal conditions

ARTICLE 110 - REQUIREMENTS FOR ELECTRICAL INSTALLATIONS
****

23. Current-carrying conductors shall be _____ unless otherwise provided in the Code.

A. stranded
B. solid
C. copper
D. aluminum

24. Electrical equipment shall be installed _____.

A. in a neat and orderly manner
B. in an orderly and workmanlike manner
C. in a neat and professional manner
D. in a neat and workmanlike manner

25. In the NEC®, conductor sizes are expressed in _____.

A. American wire Gage
B. circular mils only
C. American Wire Gage or circular mils
D. Brown and Sharp Gage

26. Connections between copper and aluminum conductors shall be _____.

A. identified for the purpose
B. prohibited
C. not allowed
D. marked AL/CUA

27. According to the NEC®, properly completed wiring systems:

A. will result in an installation that is efficient.
B. will be adequate for good service and future expansion.
C. shall be free from short circuits.
D. all of the above.

28. Connection by means of wire-binding screws or studs that have upturned lugs shall be permitted for size _____ or smaller conductors.

A. 10 AWG
B. 8 AWG
C. 6 AWG
D. 14 AWG

29. The required MINIMUM working space, in feet, for a 120/240 volt, single-phase service, when grounded parts are opposite the service is _____.

A. 2 feet
B. 2½ feet
C. 3 feet
D. 4 feet

30. Where a switchboard over 6 feet wide is installed in an electrical equipment room, and where the switchboard is rated _____ or more, under normal conditions the equipment room is required to have two (2) entrances.

A. 400 amperes
B. 800 amperes
C. 1200 amperes
D. 1600 amperes

31. The MINIMUM height of working spaces about service equipment, switchboards, panelboards, or motor control centers of 600 volts or less and 6 feet tall, shall be _____.

A. 78 inches
B. 72 inches
C. 84 inches
D. 96 inches

32. Unused openings in metal boxes, panels, and other enclosures shall be _____.

A. open
B. effectively closed
C. not required to be closed if on the bottom of the enclosure
D. not required to be closed if the enclosure is in a dry location

33. Where an industrial building is served by an outdoor 12.5 kV transformer having exposed live parts and enclosed by a fence, the fence enclosing the transformer must be at LEAST _____ high.

A. 12 feet
B. 7 feet
C. 8 feet
D. 10 feet

34. Live parts of electrical equipment operating at 50 volts or more shall be guarded against accidental contact by approved enclosures or by elevation of at LEAST _____ above the floor or other working surface.

A. 6 feet
B. 8 feet
C. 10 feet
D. 12 feet

35. A motor controller enclosure that may be subject to occasional prolonged submersion is required to be a MINIMUM enclosure type number _____.

A. 6P
B. 6
C. 3 RX
D. 3 X

36. The NEC® mandates sufficient access and working space to be provided in front of all electrical equipment for the purpose of maintenance of such equipment. The width of the working space in front of the electrical equipment shall be the width of the equipment or at LEAST _____, whichever is greater.

A. 24 inches
B. 30 inches
C. 4 feet
D. 3 feet, 6 inches

37. What is the MINIMUM dimension required by the NEC® for a working space containing live parts on both sides of the equipment that will require examination and maintenance of the equipment when energized and operating at 480 volts between conductors?

A. 3 feet
B. 4 feet
C. 5 feet
D. 6 feet

38. Electrical equipment rooms or enclosures housing electrical apparatus that are controlled by a lock(s) shall be considered accessible to _____.

A. qualified persons only
B. electricians only
C. the buildings management
D. the authority having jurisdiction

39. For subsurface enclosures such as manholes, tunnels, and vaults, all conductors and cables shall be _____ to provide ready and safe access into which persons enter for installation and maintenance.

A. racked up in an approved manner
B. at least 3 feet from the personnel opening
C. prohibited within 2 feet from the personnel opening
D. installed in conduit

40. In general, round access openings in a manhole shall NOT be less than _____ in diameter.

A. 18 inches
B. 24 inches
C. 26 inches
D. 30 inches

41. Manhole covers shall be OVER _____ in weight or otherwise require the use of tools to open.

A. 25 lbs
B. 50 lbs.
C. 75 lbs.
D. 100 lbs.

42. Where manholes and vaults have communicating openings into enclosed areas used by _____, ventilation to open air shall be provided wherever practicable.

A. authorized persons only
B. the public
C. qualified persons only
D. licensed personnel only

43. When installing electrical equipment, which of the following is NOT to be taken into consideration?

A. suitability for installation
B. mechanical strength
C. wire bending space
D. all of these must be taken into consideration

44. Electrical equipment such as switchboards, panelboards, industrial control panels, and motor control centers located in commercial and industrial occupancies are required to be field marked to warn _____ of potential electric arc flash hazards.

A. qualified persons
B. electricians
C. unqualified persons
D. the authority having jurisdiction

45. Where an equipment room houses electrical equipment rated at LEAST _____ or more, the personnel doors intended for entrance to and egress from the working space, shall open in the direction of egress.

A. 1200 amperes
B. 1500 amperes
C. 2000 amperes
D. 1800 amperes

ARTICLE 200 - USE AND IDENTIFICATION OF GROUNDED CONDUCTORS
****

46. An insulated grounded conductor of size _____ or smaller shall be identified by a continuous white or natural gray outer finish or other approved means its entire length.

A. 4 AWG
B. 6 AWG
C. 2 AWG
D. 1 AWG

47. Terminals of devices, excluding panelboards, to which a grounded conductor is to be connected shall be identified as _____ in color or other approved means.

A. white
B. green
C. copper
D. orange

48. At the time of installation, grounded (neutral) conductors larger that size 6 AWG may be indentified at its terminations by _____ colored phase tape.

A. white
B. orange
C. red
D. blue

49. In general, multiconductor flat cable of size 4 AWG or larger shall be permitted to employ an external _____ on the grounded (neutral) conductor.

A. color coding
B. marking
C. gray color
D. ridge

50. No grounded conductor shall be attached to any terminal or lead so as to _____ the designated polarity.

A. change
B. reverse
C. energize
D. ground

************************END OF UNIT ONE************************

UNIT TWO

NEC® QUESTIONS FROM ARTICLE 210

The following National Electrical Code® questions are typical of questions encountered on all electricians' exams, based on the above referenced Articles of the Code. Select the best answer from the choices given then review your answers with the answer key at the back of this book.

ARTICLE 210 – BRANCH CIRCUITS
****

1. In dwelling units, the MAXIMUM voltage permitted between conductors supplying luminaires shall NOT exceed _____.

A. 240 volts
B. 277 volts
C. 208 volts
D. 120 volts

2. Ground fault circuit interrupter (GFCI) protection MUST be provided in residential kitchens for 125-volt, 15- and 20-ampere receptacles _____.

A. always
B. that serve the countertop surface
C. that also serve the dining room
D. only if they are within six feet of the sink

3. Where the premise wiring system has branch-circuits supplied from more than one nominal voltage system, each ungrounded conductor of a branch-circuit shall be identified by _____ at the panelboard.

A. floor
B. voltage
C. phase and system
D. room

4. For household electric ranges rated 8.75 kW or more, the MINIMUM branch-circuit rating shall be _____.

A. 30 amperes
B. 40 amperes
C. 50 amperes
D. 60 amperes

5. Disregarding exceptions, a branch-circuit shall have an allowable ampacity equal to _____ percent of the noncontinuous load it serves, plus _____ percent of the continuous load it serves.

A. 80, 100
B. 125, 100
C. 80, 125
D. 100, 125

6. Where a one-family dwelling has a hallway 22 ft. in length, what is the MINIMUM number of general-use receptacles required in the hallway?

A. one
B. two
C. three
D. four

7. Information on the different types of arc-fault circuit interrupters can be found in the UL Publication _____, *Standard for Arc-Fault Circuit Interrupters*.

A. 1699-1999
B. 1999-2008
C. 1449-1992
D. 1993-2008

8. Disregarding exceptions, when an individual 20-ampere branch-circuit serves a single receptacle outlet, the rating of the receptacle must NOT be less than _____.

A. 10 amperes
B. 15 amperes
C. 16 amperes
D. 20 amperes

9. The rating of any one cord-and-plug connected appliance used on a 30-ampere rated branch-circuit shall NOT be more than _____.

A. 20 amperes
B. 24 amperes
C. 25 amperes
D. 30 amperes

10. In kitchens of dwelling units, receptacle outlets for countertop spaces shall be installed so that there is a MAXIMUM distance of _____, measured horizontally between the receptacles.

A. 21 inches
B. 24 inches
C. 6 feet
D. 4 feet

11. When a 15- or 20-ampere rated branch-circuit supplies three (3) 15-ampere rated receptacles, the MAXIMUM load any one receptacle is permitted to carry is _____.

A. 10 amperes
B. 12 amperes
C. 15 amperes
D. 8 amperes

12. All 125-volt general-use receptacles installed in the bathroom of a hotel must be _____.

   I. GFCI protected
   II. on a dedicated 20-ampere rated circuit

A. I only
B. II only
C. either I or II
D. neither I nor II

13. In a residential occupancy, how many bathroom receptacles are permitted to be installed from the garage GFCI protected receptacle?

A. none
B. one
C. two
D. unlimited

14. All conductors in a multiwire branch-circuit shall originate from the same _____.

A. feeder
B. service
C. panelboard
D. receptacle

15. Where a 125-volt receptacle is installed on a dwelling unit kitchen island countertop 8 feet from the kitchen sink, which of the following statements, if any, are correct?

A. GFCI protection is not required because the receptacle is not within 6 feet of the sink.
B. GFCI protection is required for all countertop kitchen receptacles.
C. GFCI protection is not required on receptacles installed on kitchen islands.
D. None of the above.

16. In kitchens of dwellings, receptacle outlets required for the countertop surface must be located above, but NOT more than _____ above the countertop surface.

A. 18 inches
B. 20 inches
C. 12 inches
D. 24 inches

17. Outdoor receptacles at a dwelling unit are NOT required to be GFCI protected if they are supplied from a dedicated branch-circuit and installed:

A. in a weatherproof box.
B. at a second floor level.
C. at least 6½ ft. above grade level.
D. for electric snow melting or deicing equipment and not readily accessible.

18. Duplex receptacles installed on a 120-volt, 20-ampere, small-appliance circuit in a residence are to be rated _____.

   I. 20 amperes
   II. 15 amperes

A. I only
B. II only
C. either I or II
D. neither I nor II

19. When installed in dwelling unit bedrooms, which of the following listed is/are required to be protected by an AFCI protection device?

A. receptacles
B. luminaires
C. ceiling fans
D. all of these

20. All 15- or 20-ampere, 125-volt, single-phase, receptacles installed in a residential garage must be _____.

A. provided with AFCI protection
B. provided with GFCI protection
C. provided with a metal faceplate
D. a single receptacle

21. All 120-volt, single-phase, 15- or 20-ampere rated receptacle outlets installed in the following locations of dwelling units shall be protected by a listed ground-fault circuit interrupter EXCEPT _____.

A. garages
B. bathrooms
C. hallways
D. outdoors

22. For a 15- and 20-ampere branch-circuit, the rating of any one (1) cord-and-plug-connected utilization equipment not fastened in place shall NOT exceed _____ of the branch-circuit ampere rating.

A. 80 percent
B. 70 percent
C. 60 percent
D. 50 percent

23. General-use receptacles in a dwelling located in a living room or bedroom, shall be installed such that no point measured horizontally in any wall space is more than _____ from a receptacle.

A. 10 feet
B. 8 feet
C. 6 feet
D. 12 feet

24. In a dwelling unit bedroom, any wall space that is at LEAST _____ or more in width must be provided with a general-use receptacle outlet.

A. 2 feet
B. 4 feet
C. 6 feet
D. 10 feet

25. Receptacle outlets installed in floors of dwelling units shall not be counted as part of the required number of receptacle outlets, if they are MORE than _____ from the wall.

A. 12 inches
B. 18 inches
C. 24 inches
D. 30 inches

26. A receptacle outlet shall be installed at each residential kitchen countertop space that is at LEAST _____ or wider.

A. 18 inches
B. 36 inches
C. 24 inches
D. 12 inches

27. What is the MINIMUM number of general-use receptacle outlets that must be located in a residential kitchen island with a long dimension of 48 inches and 18 inches wide?

A. none
B. one
C. two
D. three

28. In dwelling unit bathrooms, at least one GFCI protected outlet shall be installed on a wall or partition that is adjacent to the _____.

A. door
B. basin
C. toilet
D. bathtub

29. Where the heating, air-conditioning or refrigeration equipment is installed on the roof of an apartment building, a 15- or 20-ampere, 125-volt receptacle _____.

A. is not required by the Code
B. may be on the line side of the equipment disconnecting means, provided the receptacle is of the GFCI type
C. shall be located on the same level and within 25 feet of the equipment
D. may be located anywhere on the roof where the equipment is located, if the receptacle is within at least 75 feet from the equipment

30. Where a receptacle outlet is to be installed in a dwelling for the laundry equipment, the outlet shall be located within at LEAST _____ of the intended location of the appliance to be served.

A. 2 feet
B. 4 feet
C. 6 feet
D. 8 feet

31. The NEC® mandates the MINIMUM number of 20-ampere rated branch-circuits for a one-family dwelling is _____.

A. four
B. three
C. five
D. two

32. What kind of protection is required for an outdoor receptacle outlet located under the soffit of a dwelling installed for holiday lighting?

A. GFCI
B. GEPE
C. AFCI
D. standard 20 ampere rated circuit breaker

33. Where a retail store has a show window, at least one (1) receptacle outlet shall be provided for the show window lighting and installed WITHIN _____ of the top of the show window for each 12 linear feet of show window area.

A. 12 inches
B. 18 inches
C. 24 inches
D. 30 inches

34. Wall mounted 15- and 20-ampere, 125-volt receptacle outlets installed in dwelling units, shall not be counted as part of the required number of receptacle outlets where they are located MORE than _____ above the floor.

A. 18 inches
B. 24 inches
C. 5½ feet
D. 6 feet

35. In dormitories, guest rooms, and guest suites of hotels and motels, at LEAST _____ general-use receptacle outlet(s) shall be readily accessible.

A. one
B. two
C. three
D. four

36. Foyers of dwelling units, that are not part of a hallway, with an area that is at LEAST _____ or greater, shall have a general-use receptacle located in each wall space that is 3 feet or more in width.

A. 20 sq. feet
B. 40 sq. feet
C. 61 sq. feet
D. 100 sq. feet

37. In a dwelling unit, which of the following, if any, is permitted to be connected to the two (2) required 20-ampere small-appliance branch-circuits serving countertop receptacle outlets?

    I. receptacle outlet for refrigerator
    II. receptacle outlet for kitchen exhaust fan

A. I only
B. II only
C. both I and II
D. neither I nor II

38. In which of the following listed locations does the NEC® require general-use receptacle outlets to be installed?

A. clothes closets
B. crawl spaces used for storage only
C. usable attic spaces
D. attached garages

39. In what room(s) is a wall-switched receptacle outlet allowed to be used instead of a lighting outlet?

      I. hallway
      II. garage

A. I only
B. II only
C. both I and II
D. neither I nor II

40. In dwelling units, lighting and switching requirements in the NEC® require the following, if any, for crawl spaces or attics without storage or equipment.

      I. lighting outlet
      II. wall switch

A. I only
B. II only
C. both I and II
D. neither I nor II

41. One-family dwellings with direct outdoor grade level access in front and back, shall be provided with _____.

A. one receptacle at the back
B. one receptacle at the front
C. one receptacle at the front and one at the back
D. no receptacles required

42. For the kitchen small-appliance load on a dwelling unit, the MINIMUM requirement(s) is/are at LEAST _____.

A. one – 15 ampere circuit
B. two – 15 ampere circuits
C. one – 20 ampere circuit
D. two – 20 ampere circuits

43. Disregarding exceptions, where residential lighting outlets are installed in interior stairways, there shall be a wall switch _____.

A. near the stairs
B. every seven steps
C. at the top of the stairs and the bottom of the stairs if there are more than six steps
D at any convenient location

44. In dwellings, lighting outlets shall be permitted to be controlled by occupancy sensors, PROVIDED they are _____.

A. automatic
B. located in the hallway
C. within 6 feet of the door(s)
D. equipped with a manual override

45. What is the MINIMUM size branch-circuit rating when supplying more than one cord-and-plug connected portable load?

A. 10 amperes
B. 15 amperes
C. 20 amperes
D. 30 amperes

46. In general, which of the following receptacles in a commercial kitchen are required by the NEC® to be GFCI protected?

A. All 125-volt, 15- or 20-ampere rated receptacles.
B. All 125-volt, 15- or 20-ampere rated receptacles in wet locations only.
C. All receptacles.
D. All 125-volt, countertop receptacles only.

47. AFCI protection is required for all 15- and 20-ampere, 120-volt, branch-circuits supplying outlets located in _____.

A. boat houses
B. recreational vehicles
C. all guest rooms and suites of hotels
D. guest rooms and guest suites of hotels that are provided with permanent provisions for cooking

48. A basement used for storage only in a one-family dwelling is required to have _____ installed.

A. a switched lighting outlet only
B. a receptacle outlet only
C. a switched lighting outlet and a receptacle outlet
D. none of these

49. The receptacle outlet provided for a central vacuum assembly located in an attached garage of a dwelling unit is required to have _____.

A. AFCI protection
B. GFCI protection
C. LCDI protection
D. a metallic faceplate

50. When an evaporative cooler is mounted on the roof of a one-family dwelling, where is the service receptacle required to be located?

A. Within 75 feet of the cooler.
B. Within 50 feet of the cooler on the same level.
C. Within 25 feet of the cooler on the same level.
D. Not required on one-family dwelling units.

END OF UNIT TWO
****

UNIT THREE

NEC® QUESTIONS FROM ARTICLE 215 THROUGH ARTICLE 240

The following National Electrical Code® questions are typical of questions encountered on all electricians' exams, based on the above referenced Articles of the Code. Select the best answer from the choices given then review your answers with the answer key at the back of this book.

ARTICLE 215 - FEEDERS
****

1. Up to _____ sets of 3-wire feeders or two sets of 4-wire or 5-wire feeders shall be permitted to utilize a common neutral.

A. two
B. three
C. four
D. five

2. Where feeder conductors are installed in a metal raceway, all the feeder conductors using a common neutral conductor shall be:

A. of the same insulation type.
B. of the same color.
C. enclosed within the same raceway.
D. of the same polarity.

3. Where a feeder supplies continuous loads and noncontinuous loads and the overcurrent device is not listed for operation of 100 percent of its rating, the rating of the overcurrent device shall not be less than the noncontinuous load PLUS _____ of the continuous load.

A. 125 percent
B. 150 percent
C. 80 percent
D. 25 percent

4. Disregarding exceptions, which one of the following listed feeder circuits must have GFCI protection?

A. 120/240 volt, single-phase, - 1000 ampere rating
B. 208Y/120 volt, 3-phase, - 100 ampere rating
C. 480Y/277 volt, 3-phase, - 600 ampere rating
D. 480Y/277 volt, 3-phase, - 1000 ampere rating

ARTICLE 220 - BRANCH-CIRCUIT, FEEDER, and SERVICE CALCULATIONS
****

5. When doing residential service and feeder calculations, electric clothes dryers are to be calculated at a MINIMUM of _____ watts (VA), or the nameplate rating, whichever is larger.

A. 2000
B. 3000
C. 4500
D. 5000

6. When calculating the MINIMUM number of 120-volt general-purpose lighting circuits required for an apartment building that has cooking facilities provided in each unit, the calculation shall be based on _____ per sq. ft. of the outside dimensions of the building.

A. 1 VA
B. 2 VA
C. 3 VA
D. 3½ VA

7. The demand factor for an electric range which may be applied to the grounded (neutral) conductor load is _____.

A. 40 percent
B. 50 percent
C. 60 percent
D. 70 percent

8. When calculating the general lighting and general-purpose receptacle load on a bank building, and the actual number of general-purpose receptacles to be installed is yet to be determined; a unit load of _____ per sq. ft. shall be included for the receptacle outlets.

A. 0 VA
B. 1 VA
C. 2 VA
D. 3½ VA

9. A MINIMUM load of _____ for each required 120-volt, single-phase, laundry branch circuit shall be included with the general lighting load, when calculating the demand load of a one-family dwelling.

A. 1500 VA
B. 1200 VA
C. 1800 VA
D. 2400 VA

10. When applying the general method of calculation for dwelling units, the service and feeder conductor demand load for one (1) 12 kW electric range is _____.

A. 6 kW
B. 8 kW
C. 10 kW
D. 12 kW

11. When calculating the total load on a dwelling, how many VA per sq. ft. must be included for the general-use receptacles?

A. none
B. 1 VA
C. 2 VA
D. 3 VA

12. When calculating the total load on a non-dwelling occupancy, such as an office building, general-use receptacle outlets shall be computed based on a MINIMUM of _____ per duplex receptacle.

A. 100 VA
B. 150 VA
C. 180 VA
D. 200 VA

13. Where applying the general (standard) method of calculation for a one-family dwelling, it shall be permissible to apply a demand factor of _____ to the nameplate rating of four (4) or more fixed appliances, other than ranges, dryers, and heating and air conditioning equipment when calculating the electrical demand load of the house.

A. 75 percent
B. 70 percent
C. 60 percent
D. 50 percent

14. For circuits supplying lighting units that have ballasts, transformers, or LED drivers, the calculated load shall be based on _____.

A. the total watts of the lamp
B. the total VA of the lamps
C. 125% of the total watts of the lamp
D. the total amperage ratings of the lighting units

15. When sizing the service entrance conductors for a farm service, the second largest load of the total load, shall be calculated at _____.

A. 90 percent
B. 80 percent
C. 75 percent
D. 65 percent

ARTICLE 225 - OUTSIDE BRANCH CIRCUITS and FEEDERS
****

16. Overhead spans of outside open conductors of not over 600 volts, over an apple orchard or an orange grove, shall have a MINIMUM clearance from ground of _____.

A. 10 feet
B. 12 feet
C. 15 feet
D. 18 feet

17. Outside open conductors of not over 600 volts shall have a clearance of NOT less than _____ from signs, chimneys, and TV antennas.

A. 3 feet
B. 12 feet
C. 6 feet
D. 8 feet

18. Unless supported by a messenger wire, outside overhead copper conductors with spans of 100 feet, operating at 600 volts or less, must NOT be sized smaller than _____.

A. 6 AWG
B. 8 AWG
C. 10 AWG
D. 12 AWG

19. Where an outside overhead span of 3-phase, 480Y/277 volt conductors are to be installed between two buildings and the area the conductors cross will not be subject to truck traffic, the conductors must have a MINIMUM clearance of _____ from final grade.

A. 10 feet
B. 12 feet
C. 15 feet
D. 18 feet

20. Outside branch-circuits that supply only limited loads of a single branch-circuit, are required to have a disconnecting means with a rating of NOT less than _____.

A. 15 amperes
B. 20 amperes
C. 30 amperes
D. 50 amperes

ARTICLE 230 - SERVICES
****

21. Unless otherwise permitted, a building or other structure shall be supplied by a MAXIMUM of _____ service(s).

A. one
B. two
C. six
D. unlimited

22. The point of attachment of a service-drop to a building where the voltage is 120 volts to ground shall be a MINIMUM of _____ above grade.

A. 8 feet
B. 10 feet
C. 12 feet
D. 15 feet

23. Which of the following listed wiring methods is approved for use for the service-entrance conductors where the applied voltage is 600 volts or less?

A. Type NM cable
B. Type UF cable
C. Type MC cable
D. Type FC cable

24. The service disconnecting means for a one-family dwelling shall have a rating of NOT less than _____, where 120/240 volts, single-phase.

A. 60 amperes
B. 100 amperes
C. 150 amperes
D. 200 amperes

25. Which of the following listed conductors are permitted by the NEC® to be installed in the same raceway with the service-entrance conductors?

A. bonding jumpers
B. sub-panel feeders
C. branch-circuit conductors
D. All of these

26. A building with a 480Y/277 volt, 3-phase electrical system, may be permitted to have more than one service where _____.

   I. the building is of a large area
   II. the capacity requirements of the building are in excess of 2000 amperes

A. I only
B. II only
C. either I or II
D. neither I nor II

27. Where a service disconnecting means consists of two or three single-pole switches or circuit breakers, they are required to be _____.

A. listed
B. removed
C. equipped with identified handle ties
D. linked together using a galvanized nail or similar galvanized object

28. Disregarding exceptions, underground service-lateral conductors shall NOT be smaller than _____ copper.

A. 8 AWG
B. 6 AWG
C. 4 AWG
D. 2 AWG

29. Where a service mast is constructed of rigid metal conduit (RMC) and used for the support of service-drop conductors, the NEC® requires the conduit to be of adequate strength OR be _____.

A. a minimum of 2 inches in diameter
B. a minimum of 3 inches in diameter
C. supported by braces and guys
D. less than 3 feet in height

30. The smallest service-drop conductors permissible for a limited-load, single-branch circuit is _____.

A. 6 AWG
B. 8 AWG
C. 10 AWG
D. 12 AWG

31. When a conduit containing service-entrance conductors runs beneath a building, what is the MINIMUM depth of concrete required to cover the conduit for it to be considered "outside" the building?

A. 2 inches
B. 6 inches
C. 18 inches
D. 24 inches

32. In general, in a multiple-occupancy building, each occupant shall have access to the occupant's service disconnecting means, an exception to this rule is where the electrical service and maintenance are provided and supervised by the building management, then the service disconnecting means shall be permitted to be accessible to _____.

A. licensed electricians only
B. the authority having jurisdiction
C. qualified persons only
D. authorized management personnel only

33. Which of the following listed services MUST have GFCI protection?

A. 120/240 volts, single-phase - rated 1000 amperes
B. 208Y/120 volts, 3-phase - rated 100 amperes
C. 480Y/277 volts, 3-phase - rated 600 amperes
D. 480Y/277 volts, 3-phase - rated 1000 amperes

34. For either overhead or underground primary distribution systems exceeding 600 volts on private property, the service disconnecting means shall be _____.

A. permitted to be located in a location that is not readily accessible
B. in a location that is readily accessible
C. installed at a height not exceeding 6 ft., 7 in.
D. readily accessible to qualified persons only

35. When type SE cable is installed for service-entrance conductors for an overhead service, it shall be supported WITHIN _____ of the service head and at intervals NOT exceeding _____.

A. 12 inches – 36 inches
B. 12 inches – 30 inches
C. 24 inches – 24 inches
D. 18 inches – 30 inches

36. Where a service riser contains THWN insulated conductors of 600 volts or less, is located outdoors on an exterior wall, the riser _____.

A. shall be a rigid metal conduit (RMC)
B. is permitted to be electrical metallic tubing (EMT)
C. shall be PVC conduit
D. is required to be liquidtight flexile metal conduit (LFMC)

37. Disregarding exceptions, an overhead service-drop shall have a MINIMUM clearance laterally of _____ from windows designed to be opened, doors, balconies, ladders or similar locations.

A. 2 feet
B. 3 feet
C. 6 feet
D. 10 feet

38. Where the service of a building is provided with ground-fault protection, the MAXIMIM trip time delay shall be _____ for ground-fault currents equal to or greater than 3,000 amperes.

A. one second
B. five seconds
C. thirty seconds
D. one minute

39. Where a dwelling unit has a main disconnecting means rated for 200 amperes and the calculated demand load is only 100 amperes, the ungrounded service-entrance conductors are required to have an ampacity of at LEAST _____.

A. 100 amperes
B. 125 amperes
C. 150 amperes
D. 200 amperes

40. The service disconnect for each service shall consist of NOT more than _____ switches or circuit breakers.

A. one
B. two
C. four
D. six

ARTICLE 240 - OVERCURRENT PROTECTION
****

41. Which one of the following listed is NOT a standard ampere rating for circuit breakers?

A. 75 amperes
B. 90 amperes
C. 110 amperes
D. 175 amperes

42. Where a busway has an ampere rating of 1,100 amperes, what is the MAXIMUM standard size overcurrent protection devices that may be used to protect the busway?

A. 1,100 amperes
B. 1,200 amperes
C. 900 amperes
D. 1,000 amperes

43. Where the allowable ampacity of a conductor that is not part of a multioutlet branch-circuit or a motor branch-circuit, is determined to be 55 amperes, what is the MAXIMIM standard size overcurrent protection device that may be used to protect the circuit?

A. 50 amperes
B. 55 amperes
C. 60 amperes
D. 40 amperes

44. In dwelling units, panelboards that house overcurrent devices shall NOT be located:

   I. in bathrooms.
   II. in the vicinity of easily ignitible material, such as clothes closets.

A. I only
B. II only
C. both I and II
D. neither I nor II

45. Where the sub-feeder conductors less than ten (10) feet long are tapped from feeder conductors, the ampacity of the tap conductors shall be _____.

A. one-half of the rating of the overcurrent device protecting the feeder conductors
B. one-third of the rating of the overcurrent device protecting the feeder conductors
C. 125 percent of the combined loads to be served by the tap conductors
D. not less than the combined calculated loads on the circuits supplied by the tap conductors

46. Plug fuses of 15-ampere and lower rating, shall be identified by a/an _____.

A. clear window or cap
B. octagon configuration or cap
C. white window or cap
D. hexagon configuration window or cap

47. The largest standard rating for an inverse time circuit breaker is _____.

A. 400 amperes
B. 600 amperes
C. 1200 amperes
D. 6000 amperes

48. Where a feeder tap is made at a high bay manufacturing building, overcurrent protection at the tap is not required if the tap conductors are not over 100 feet in total length and the tap is made NO less than _____ from the floor.

A. 25 feet
B. 30 feet
C. 35 feet
D. 50 feet

49. Edison base fuses are prohibited _____.

A. for new work in all buildings
B. in commercial occupancies for existing work
C. in residential occupancies for replacement only
D. in damp locations

50. When circuit breakers are used to switch 120-volt and 277-volt fluorescent lighting branch-circuits, the circuit breakers shall be listed and marked_____.

   I. SWD
   II. HID

A. I only
B. II only
C. either I or II
D. both I and II

END OF UNIT THREE

UNIT FOUR

NEC® QUESTIONS FROM ARTICLE 250

The following National Electrical Code® questions are typical of questions encountered on all electricians' exams, based on the above referenced Articles of the Code. Select the best answer from the choices given then review your answers with the answer key at the back of this book.

ARTICLE 250 - GROUNDING
****

1. The grounded service-entrance conductor shall NOT be smaller than the required:

A. grounding electrode conductor.
B. largest phase conductor.
C. ungrounded service entrance conductor.
D. largest feeder conductor.

2. A metal underground water pipe may serve as a grounding electrode if it is in direct contact with the earth for at LEAST _____ or more.

A. 6 feet
B. 8 feet
C. 10 feet
D. 12 feet

3. A connection to a concrete encased driven or buried grounding electrode shall _____.

A. be accessible
B. not be required to be accessible
C. not permitted to be buried
D. be visible

4. A ground rod is required to be driven a MINIMUM of _____ into the soil.

A. 4 feet
B. 6 feet
C. 8 feet
D. 10 feet

5. Which one of the following listed is prohibited for connection of a grounding conductor to equipment?

A. sheet metal screws
B. pressure connectors
C. clamps
D. lugs

6. Which of the following does the NEC® prohibit to be used as a grounding electrode?

A. A metal underground gas pipe.
B. A metal underground water pipe.
C. A 3/4 in. metal conduit, 10 ft. in length.
D. The metal frame of a building.

7. According to the NEC®, ferrous metal enclosures for grounding electrode conductors shall be _____.

A. electrically continuous
B. isolated
C. prohibited
D. watertight

8. The NEC® mandates stainless steel ground rods that are not listed, to be NOT less than _____ in diameter.

A. 1/2 in.
B. 3/4 in.
C. 5/8 in.
D. 7/8 in.

9. Where used outside, aluminum or copper-clad aluminum grounding conductors shall NOT be terminated within _____ of the earth.

A. 1½ feet
B. 2 feet
C. 3 feet
D. 6 feet

10. Where required, the MINIMUM size copper equipment grounding conductor to electrical equipment supplied by a 40 ampere branch-circuit is _____.

A. 8 AWG
B. 10 AWG
C. 12 AWG
D. 14 AWG

11. What is the smallest trade size rigid metal conduit (RMC) that may be used as a grounding electrode?

A. 1/2 in.
B. 5/8 in.
C. 3/4 in.
D. 1 in.

12. Where ungrounded conductors of a circuit are adjusted to compensate for voltage drop, equipment grounding conductors where installed, shall be adjusted proportionally according to _____.

A. diameter
B. cross-sectional area
C. circular mil area
D. circumference

13. What is the purpose of an equipment grounding conductor?

A. To reduce voltage drop.
B. To limit galvanic corrosion.
C. To reduce electrolysis.
D. To establish an effective ground-fault path and facilitate the operation of the overcurrent protective device.

14. The NEC® mandates the grounding electrode conductor to be connected to the grounded service conductor _____.

A. within 5 ft. of the service equipment on the load side
B. at any point on the load side of the service disconnecting means
C. at the subpanel outside the building
D. at any accessible point on the load side of the service drop or service lateral

15. An intersystem bonding termination for connecting intersystem bonding and grounding conductors required for other systems, shall be _____ at the service equipment or metering equipment.

A. provided internally in enclosures
B. provided external to enclosures
C. mounted on the enclosure
D. installed at a height of not more than 6 feet

16. Each grounding electrode plate shall expose NOT less than _____ of surface area to the exterior soil.

A. 1 sq. ft.
B. 1½ sq. ft.
C. 2 sq. ft.
D. 3 sq. ft.

17. Where installed on the exterior side of a building, short sections of metal raceways used to protect cables from physical damage _____.

A. shall be required to be grounded
B. shall not be required to be connected to the equipment grounding conductor
C. are prohibited
D. are required to be a minimum trade size ¾ in.

18. Where a commercial electrical service consists of size 3/0 AWG copper service-entrance conductors and is to be connected to the building steel that is used as the grounding electrode, the grounding electrode conductor shall NOT be smaller than _____.

A. 2 AWG
B. 4 AWG
C. 6 AWG
D. 8 AWG

19. What is the MINIMUM size copper equipment grounding conductor required for a raceway containing the following group of branch-circuits? One (1) 30 ampere, two (2) 20 ampere, and two (2) 50 ampere.

A. 4 AWG
B. 6 AWG
C. 8 AWG
D. 10 AWG

20. The MINIMUM size copper wire that may be used for grounding the secondary of an instrument transformer is _____.

A. 8 AWG
B. 10 AWG
C. 12 AWG
D. 14 AWG

21. Where the only grounding electrode available for a 400 ampere rated temporary service is a driven ground rod, what is the MINIMUM size copper grounding electrode conductor permitted by the NEC®?

A. 6 AWG
B. 4 AWG
C. 2 AWG
D. 1/0 AWG

22. Where a 500 ampere service is supplied by two (2) parallel size 350 kcmil aluminum conductors per phase, the NEC® mandates a MINIMUM size copper grounding electrode conductor of _____ to be connected to the cold water pipe used as the grounding electrode.

A. 2 AWG
B. 1/0 AWG
C. 2/0 AWG
D. 3/0 AWG

23. With respect to the service disconnecting means, the grounding electrode conductor shall be connected to the grounded service conductor on _____.

A. both supply and load sides
B. either supply or load side
C. the load side
D. the supply side

24. A concrete encased grounding electrode encased in at least a 2 inches of concrete shall NOT be smaller than size_____ bare copper conductor.

A. 4 AWG
B. 6 AWG
C. 8 AWG
D. 10 AWG

25. Where multiple driven ground rods are installed, they shall NOT be less than _____ apart.

A. 18 inches
B. 3 feet
C. 6 feet
D. 8 feet

26. When a grounding ring consist of size 2 AWG bare copper wire encircling a building, buried 36 in. deep, in direct contact with the earth, what is the MINIMUM length of the wire permitted for the grounding electrode in this ground ring?

A. 15 feet
B. 20 feet
C. 25 feet
D. 50 feet

27. Which of the following statements is true for grounding and bonding of metal gas lines?

A. A buried natural gas line may be used as an electrical systems only grounding electrode.
B. A buried natural gas line may be used as a grounding electrode when supplemented by another electrode.
C. The furnace gas line must be bonded to an electrical system.
D. An interior gas line may be used as an equipment grounding conductor.

28. Which one of the following grounding electrodes must be supplemented by an additional electrode?

A. metal underground water pipe
B. ground ring
C. metal frame of a building
D. concrete encased

29. Where the metal frame of the building is used as the grounding electrode, at least one structural member must be in direct contact with the earth for _____ or more.

A. 5 feet
B. 6 feet
C. 8 feet
D. 10 feet

30. The connection of a grounding electrode is required by the NEC® to be accessible:

   I. when connected to a water pipe installed above ground.
   II. when connected to a driven ground rod.

A. I only
B. II only
C. both I and II
D. neither I nor II

31. As per the NEC®, grounding electrode conductors sized at 8 AWG shall be installed in a protective raceway. Raceways approved by the NEC® are _____.

A. rigid metal conduit (RMC)
B. polyvinyl chloride conduit (PVC)
C. electrical metallic tubing (EMT)
D. all of these listed

32. Where ungrounded conductors are run in parallel in multiple raceways, the equipment grounding conductor, where used, shall be _____.

A. insulated
B. installed in parallel in each raceway
C. installed in one raceway only
D. uninsulated

33. Disregarding exceptions, where an ac system operating at LESS than _____ is grounded at any point, the grounded conductor shall be run to each service disconnecting means and shall be connected to each disconnecting means grounded conductor(s) terminal or bus.

A. 300 volts
B. 600 volts
C. 480 volts
D. 1000 volts

34. The bonding of circuits of over 250 volts to ground shall be ensured by installing the conductors in _____.

A. threaded rigid metal conduit (RMC) and using double locknuts
B. PVC conduit and isolating the grounding conductors
C. threaded rigid metal conduit (RMC) and using insulated bushings
D. PVC conduit and using insulated bushings

35. As long as it has continuity to the grounding electrode system, an equipment grounding conductor may be _____.

A. steel conduit
B. the building steel structure member
C. the building metallic water system
D. any of the above

36. The National Electrical Code® requires equipment grounding conductors to be:

   I. green in color or bare.
   II. white or gray in color.

A. I only
B. II only
C. either I or II
D. neither I nor II

37. Where installed on the outside of a raceway, the length of the equipment bonding jumper shall NOT exceed _____ and shall be routed with the raceway.

A. 3 feet
B. 4 feet
C. 6 feet
D. 10 feet

38. The lightning protection system grounding terminals shall be bonded to _____.

A. the grounded terminal bar at the main disconnecting means
B. the ungrounded terminal bar at the main disconnecting means
C. the building of structure grounding electrode system
D. none of these, it shall be isolated from the building or structure

39. The MINIMUM length of a driven ground rod shall NOT be less than _____.

A. 4 feet
B. 6 feet
C. 8 feet
D. 10 feet

40. Grounding electrode conductors for services are to be sized in reference to _____.

A. the largest service-entrance conductor
B. the size of the grounded conductors
C. the rating of the overcurrent protection
D. the type of grounding electrode to be used

41. Grounding electrodes of _____ shall NOT be permitted.

A. aluminum
B. stainless steel
C. galvanized pipe
D. all of these

42. The bonding jumper for service raceways are to be sized according to the _____.

A. load to be served
B. service conductor size
C. service-drop conductors from the utility company
D. calculated load after taking demand factors into consideration

43. Listed flexible metal conduit (FMC) is approved for use as an equipment grounding conductor where the FMC is not longer than 6 ft. and the circuit conductors contained in the FMC are protected by overcurrent devices rated NOT more than _____.

A. 15 amperes
B. 20 amperes
C. 30 amperes
D. 40 amperes

44. When driving a ground rod and encounter solid rock which prevents you from installing the ground rod the required depth of 8 feet, which of the following methods of installation, if any, is permitted by the NEC®?

    I. Cut the ground rod in 4 ft. lengths and install each section at least 6 ft. apart.
    II. Bury the ground rod in a trench at least 2 ft. deep.

A. I only
B. II only
C. either I or II
D. neither I nor II

45. What other purpose is permitted by the NEC® for a grounding screw in a metal box that is being used to connect the grounding conductor?

A. Connecting the grounded conductor.
B. Support for cable clamps.
C. Connecting extension rings.
D. The NEC® permits no other purpose.

46. Where two (2) or more driven ground rods form the entire grounding electrode system of a building or structure, what is the MAXIMUM size copper conductor required to bond the ground rods together, regardless of the size of the service?

A. 8 AWG
B. 6 AWG
C. 4 AWG
D. 2 AWG

47. Where installed in or at a building or structure, the same _____ is required to be used for the grounding of all ac systems where the building or structure is provided with more than one service.

A. grounding electrode
B. grounded raceway
C. bonding jumper
D. electrode enclosure

48. In general, a grounding electrode conductor for a separately derived system is required to be connected to the nearest available _____.

    I. structural metal grounding electrode
    II. metal water pipe grounding electrode

A. I only
B. II only
C. either I or II
D. both I and II

49. A single made electrode, such as a driven ground rod, shall have a resistance to ground of _____.

A. 25 ohms or more
B. 50 ohms or less
C. 25 ohms or less
D. 50 ohms or more

50. The interior metal water piping system of a building shall be bonded to the _____.

A. service equipment enclosure
B. grounded conductor at the service
C. grounding electrode conductor
D. all of the above

END OF UNIT FOUR
****

UNIT FIVE

NEC® QUESTIONS FROM ARTICLE 300 THROUGH ARTICLE 310

The following National Electrical Code® questions are typical of questions encountered on all electricians' exams, based on the above referenced Articles of the Code. Select the best answer from the choices given then review your answers with the answer key at the back of this book.

ARTICLE 300 - WIRING METHODS
****

1. A metal box or terminal fitting having separately bushed holes for each conductor, shall be used whenever change is made from conduit to _____.

A. nonmetallic cable
B. type AC cable
C. type MC cable
D. knob-and-tube wiring

2. What is the MINIMUM burial depth of intermediate metal conduit (IMC) containing conductors of 600 volts or less, under a residential gravel driveway, where GFCI protection is not provided?

A. 6 inches
B. 12 inches
C. 18 inches
D. 24 inches

3. Given: Type UF cable is to be used for direct-buried residential branch-circuits of 120 volts. The conductors are GFCI protected and overcurrent protection is rated 20 amperes; the cables do not cross under any driveways or concrete. What is the MINIMUM permitted burial depth of the cable?

A. 6 inches
B. 12 inches
C. 18 inches
D. 24 inches

4. An underground run of conduit or direct-buried cables, of not over 600 volts, in or under an airport runway, tarmac, or concourse shall be buried a MINIMUM depth of _____.

A. 1½ feet
B. 2 feet
C. 1 feet
D. 6 inches

5. Wiring in ducts of commercial cooking equipment shall be _____.

A. in rigid metal conduit (RMC)
B. Type MC cable
C. in flexible metal conduit (FMC)
D. prohibited

6. When electrical wiring passes into or through fire-resistant-rated walls, partitions, floors, or ceilings, openings around the electrical penetrations shall be_____.

A. sleeved
B. firestopped
C. shielded
D. provided with explosion-proof seals

7. A _____ shall be used at the end of a conduit that terminates underground where the conductors emerge as a direct burial wiring method.

A. compression type fitting
B. bushing
C. watertight type fitting
D. raintight type fitting

8. Unless protection is provided, when installing Type NM cable through bored holes in wooden studs, the holes shall be bored so that the edge of the hole is NOT less than _____ from the outside edge of the wooden stud.

A. 3/4 inch
B. 1 inch
C. 1¼ inches
D. 1½ inches

9. Metal conduit installed in indoor wet locations must have a MINUMUM airspace clearance of _____ between the conduit and the wall or supporting surface.

A. 1/8 inch
B. 1/4 inch
C. 1/2 inch
D. 3/8 inch

10. Where direct-buried conductors emerge from below grade and extend up a pole, the conductors must be protected by raceways up to a height of 8 feet above finished grade and in no case shall the protection be required to exceed _____ below finished grade.

A. 18 inches
B. 12 inches
C. 24 inches
D. 36 inches

11. Where conductors carrying alternating current are installed in ferrous metal raceways, _____.

A. all phase conductors, the grounded conductor and equipment grounding conductors shall be grouped together
B. the phase conductors shall not be grouped with grounded conductor
C. the equipment grounding conductor is not permitted to be in the same raceway with the grounded and ungrounded conductors
D. the equipment grounding conductors are not permitted to be installed in a common raceway with the grounded conductors

12. In general, conductors in raceways must be _____ between outlet boxes and there shall be no splice or tap within a raceway itself.

A. continuous
B. installed
C. copper
D. solid

13. Underground direct-buried service-lateral conductors shall be _____.

A. back-filled with sand only
B. wrapped with friction tape
C. protection from damage using pressure-treated board strips
D. protected from damage due to ground movement using "S" loops

14. Which of the following circuits are prohibited for the grounded conductor to be dependent upon receptacle devices for continuity?

A. all circuits
B. multi-outlet branch-circuits
C. GFCI protected circuits
D. multiwire branch-circuits

15. Where a vertical raceway contains three (3) size 3/0 AWG copper conductors, the conductors shall be supported at the top and at intervals NOT greater than _____.

A. 30 feet
B. 60 feet
C. 80 feet
D. 40 feet

16. In general, cables or raceways shall be permitted to be laid in notches in wood studs where the cables or raceways at those points are protected against nails or screws by a steel plate at LEAST _____ thick.

A. 1/16 inch
B. 1/8 inch
C. 1/4 inch
D. 3/8 inch

17. The reason the NEC® requires all phase conductors of an alternating current electrical system to be in the same ferrous metal raceway is to reduce _____.

A. expense
B. inductive heat
C. voltage drop
D. resistance

18. At LEAST _____ of free conductor, measured from the point in the box where it emerges from its raceway or cable sheath, shall be left at each outlet box, switch box, and junction box for splices or to connect to luminaires and devices.

A. 3 inches
B. 4 inches
C. 5 inches
D. 6 inches

19. In general, direct-buried cables of 13,000 volts must be buried at a depth of NOT less than _____.

A. 24 inches
B. 30 inches
C. 36 inches
D. 42 inches

20. Underground service conductors that are not encased in concrete and are buried 18 inches or more below grade shall have their location identified by a warning ribbon placed at LEAST _____ above the underground installation.

A. 6 inches
B. 8 inches
C. 12 inches
D. 24 inches

21. Where conduit is installed on the exterior wall of a building, the interior of these raceways shall be considered to be a _____.

A. dry location
B. damp location
C. wet location
D. moist location

22. Where an electrical metallic tubing (EMT) is installed in exposed or concealed locations under metal-corrugated sheet roof decking, a distance of at LEAST _____ must be maintained from the nearest surface of the roof decking to the top of the EMT.

A. 3/4 inch
B. 1 inch
C. 1¼ inch
D. 1½ inch

23. In general, when conductors of different insulation rating are installed in a common raceway and the voltage is 600 volts or less, the NEC® mandates:

A. the maximum operating voltage not to exceed the insulation rating of the lowest insulation rating of any conductor in the raceway.
B. the conduit allowable fill to be limited to 10 percent.
C. the conductors of separate ratings to be grouped and bound.
D. the insulation of the lower rated conductors to be identified with blue or yellow colors.

24. Disregarding exceptions, where raceways containing insulated conductors of size _____ or larger enter a box or cabinet, the conductors must be provided with an insulating bushing.

A. 10 AWG
B. 8 AWG
C. 6 AWG
D. 4 AWG

25. All metallic switchgear rated for over 600 volts shall be provided with a grounding busbar for the purpose of connecting the _____.

A. grounded conductors
B. metallic shield of cables
C. metal raceways
D. ungrounded conductors

26. Size 18 AWG communication conductors or cables installed in vertical raceways shall be supported at intervals NOT exceeding _____.

A. 30 feet
B. 60 feet
C. 75 feet
D. 100 feet

27. Relay control-circuit conductors associated with an ac motor rated 600 volts or more, _____.

A. shall be blue in color
B. are required to be run in the same raceway or enclosure with the motor conductors
C. shall not occupy the same enclosure with the motor-circuit conductors
D. are permitted to occupy the same enclosure with the motor-circuit conductors

28. In other spaces used for environmental air-handling purposes as a plenum, such as the space above a suspended ceiling, which of these wiring methods is NOT allowed?

A. Type MC cable without an overall nonmetallic covering
B. Type AC cable
C. rigid metal conduit (RMC)
D. liquidtight flexible metal conduit (LFMC)

ARTICLE 310 - CONDUCTORS for GENERAL WIRING
****

29. A neutral conductor is to be considered a current-carrying conductor when _____.

   I. the conductor carries only the unbalanced current from other conductors of the same circuit
   II. the major portion of the load to be served consists of nonlinear loads

A. I only
B. II only
C. both I and II
D. neither I nor II

30. When current-carrying conductors are installed in parallel, they must be _____.

   I. the same length
   II. of the same conductor material

A. I only
B. II only
C. both I and II
D. neither I nor II

31. Type XHHW insulated conductors may be used in _____.

A. dry locations only
B. wet locations only
C. dry or damp locations only
D. dry, damp, or wet locations

32. Where a one-family dwelling is supplied with a 120/240 volt, single-phase service, and the computed load after demand factors have been taken into consideration is 175 amperes, what is the MINIMUM size THWN aluminum ungrounded (phase) conductors permitted for use as service-entrance conductors?

A. 1/0 AWG
B. 2/0 AWG
C. 3/0 AWG
D. 4/0 AWG

33. Disregarding exceptions, what is the largest insulated solid conductor permitted by the NEC® to be installed in an existing raceway?

A. 4 AWG
B. 6 AWG
C. 8 AWG
D. 10 AWG

34. Which of the following conductor insulation types listed is NOT suitable for use in wet locations, such as conduit that is placed in a concrete slab that is directly in contact with the soil?

A. TW
B. THHN
C. THWN
D. XHHW

35. Where a raceway 100 feet in length encloses nine (9) current-carrying conductors, what is the derating factor which must be applied to the ampacity of these conductors?

A. 80 percent
B. 70 percent
C. 60 percent
D. 50 percent

36. Where a 25 ft. run of electrical metallic tubing (EMT) encloses three (3) current carrying size 2 AWG THW copper conductors, installed where the expected ambient temperature is 125 deg. F, the temperature correction factor that must be applied is _____.

A. 0.67
B. 0.82
C. 0.75
D. 0.76

37. Where six (6) current-carrying conductors are installed in a common conduit that is 19 inches in length, the ampacity of each conductor shall be adjusted by a factor of _____.

A. 80 percent
B. 70 percent
C. 60 percent
D. none required

38. Which of the following listed conductors have flame-retardant, moisture-resistant, thermoset insulation?

A. TW
B. TFE
C. RHW
D. RUH

39. What is the MAXIMUM allowable ampacity of a size 6 AWG THW copper conductor installed on open wiring on insulators where the ambient temperature is 86° F?

A. 65 amperes
B. 75 amperes
C. 80 amperes
D. 95 amperes

40. Which of the following listed conductor insulations are oil resistant?

A. TW
B. TFW
C. THWN
D. MTW

41. Conductors with _____ insulation have a greater ampacity when used in a dry location compared to when used in a wet location.

A. THW
B. RHW
C. THHW
D. THWN

42. The NEC® mandates a conductor may not be used if the operating temperature exceeds that allowed for the type of _____ of the wire.

A. color
B. insulation
C. conducting material
D. all of these apply

Copyright 2016   BrownTechnical.org

43. In general, when installing ungrounded (phase) conductors in parallel, they shall be of size _____ or larger.

A. 1/0 AWG
B. 2/0 AWG
C. 2 AWG
D. 8 AWG

44. Where conductors or cables are installed in conduits exposed to direct sunlight within four (4) inches above a rooftop, a temperature adder of _____ must be applied to the applicable correction factors of Table 310.15(B)(2)(a) of the NEC® to determine the allowable ampacity of the conductors.

A. 25° F
B. 30° F
C. 40° F
D. 50° F

45. Sectioned equipment grounding conductors smaller than 1/0 AWG are permitted to be installed in parallel within multiconductor cables, provided the combined circular mil area complies with _____ of the NEC®.

A. Section 310.104
B. Table 310.15(B)(16)
C. Section 250.66
D. Section 250.112

46. When multiple nonmetallic sheathed cables, Type NM, are bundled together for at LEAST _____ or more, the allowable ampacity of each conductor in the cables shall be reduced as shown in Table 310.15(B)(3)(a) of the NEC®.

A. 12 inches
B. 18 inches
C. 24 inches
D. 36 inches

47. Where a conductor is marked *RHW-2* on the insulation, what does the -2 represent?

A. The cable has 2 conductors.
B. The conductor is double insulated.
C. The conductor has a nylon outer jacket.
D. The conductor has a maximum operating temperature of 90 deg. C.

48. Where used as service-entrance conductors for a house having a 120/240 volt, single-phase electrical system, what is the maximum allowable ampacity of size 1 AWG THWN copper conductors?

A. 130 amperes
B. 150 amperes
C. 110 amperes
D. 175 amperes

49. What is the MINIMUM size 75 deg. C rated copper service-entrance conductors required for a 200 ampere rated commercial service?

A. 4/0 THW
B. 2/0 THW
C. 3/0 THHN
D. 3/0 THW

50. Thermoplastic insulated wire shall be durably marked indicating the AWG size or circular mil area on the wire surface at intervals NOT exceeding _____.

A. 24 inches
B. 18 inches
C. 30 inches
D. 36 inches

END OF UNIT FIVE

UNIT SIX

NEC® QUESTIONS FROM ARTICLE 314 THROUGH 332

The following National Electrical Code® questions are typical of questions encountered on all electricians' exams, based on the above referenced Articles of the Code. Select the best answer from the choices given then review your answers with the answer key at the back of this book.

ARTICLE 314 - OUTLET, DEVICE, PULL and JUNCTION BOXES; CONDUIT BODIES; FITTINGS; and MANHOLES
****

1. The front edge of a switch box installed in a wall constructed of wood shall be _____ from the surface of the wall.

A. flush with or project therefrom
B. set back a maximum of 1/4 in.
C. set back a maximum of 1/2 in.
D. set back a maximum of 3/8 in.

2. For the purpose of determining conductor fill in an outlet box, a luminaire stud is considered the equivalent of how many conductors?

A. none
B. one
C. two
D. three

3. Where there are two (2) internal cable clamps contained in a metal box, the number of conductors allowed in the box shall be reduced by _____ conductor(s).

A. none
B. one
C. two
D. three

4. For the purpose of determining conductor fill in a device box, the NEC® mandates a switch is to be counted as equal to two (2) conductors. The volume allowance for the two (2) conductors shall be based on _____.

A. the largest wire in the box
B. the largest grounding conductor in the box
C. the largest wire connected to the switch
D. the number of clamps in the box

5. When nails are used to fasten metal boxes to wooden studs and the nails pass through the interior of the box, the nails shall be WITHIN _____ of the back of the box.

A. 1/4 inch
B. 1/2 inch
C. 3/8 inch
D. 3/4 inch

6. When a pull box contains conductors of size 4 AWG or larger and a straight pull of the conductors are to be made, the length of the box shall NOT be less than _____ times the trade diameter of the largest conduit entering the box.

A. four
B. six
C. ten
D. eight

7. Where NM cable is installed in a nonmetallic box no larger than 2¼ in. by 4 in., the NM cable is not required to be secured to the box if the cable is fastened within at LEAST of _____ of the nonmetallic box.

A. 12 in.
B. 6 in.
C. 1½ ft.
D. 8 in.

8. When using wood braces to support metal boxes to structures, the braces shall have a cross-section of NOT less than _____.

A. 1½ in. x 3½ in.
B. 1¼ in. x 3½ in.
C. 1 in. x 2½ in.
D. 1 in. x 2 in.

9. The MINIMUM internal depth permitted of an outlet box that does not enclose devices is _____.

A. 1¼ in.
B. 1½ in.
C. 1/2 in.
D. 15/16 in.

10. Disregarding exceptions, cast junction boxes not over 100 cubic inches that have threaded entries and contain devices shall be considered adequately supported where two (2) or more conduits are threaded wrenchtight into the box and where each conduit is supported within at LEAST _____ of the box.

A. 12 inches
B. 18 inches
C. 24 inches
D. 30 inches

11. Boxes that enclose utilization equipment, supplied by 12 AWG or 10 AWG conductors, that projects more than one (1) inch rearward from the mounting plane of the box shall have a depth that is NOT less than the depth of the equipment plus _____.

A. 1/2 inch
B. 1/4 inch
C. 3/8 inch
D. 3/4 inch

12. When determining conductor fill in an outlet box, what volume allowance, in cubic inches, is required for each size 10 AWG wire in the box?

A. 2.25 cu. in.
B. 2.00 cu. in.
C. 2.50 cu. in.
D. 3.00 cu. in.

13. A 3½ in. deep masonry box that contains no devices or clamps may contain a MAXIMUM of _____ size 12 AWG conductors.

A. eight
B. six
C. seven
D. nine

14. Noncombustible surfaces that are damaged around boxes having a flush-type cover or faceplate shall be repaired so there will be no gaps greater than _____ at the edge of the box.

A. 1/8 in.
B. 1/4 in.
C. 3/8 in.
D. 1/2 in.

15. A luminaire (lighting fixture) that weighs MORE than _____ shall be supported independently of a ceiling mounted outlet box, unless the outlet box is listed and marked for the maximum weight to be supported.

A. 23 lbs.
B. 6 lbs.
C. 50 lbs.
D. 35 lbs.

16. For the purpose of determining conductor fill in a device box, where a device is more than two (2) inches wide and must fit in a 2-gang box, the device is considered to be equal to _____ conductors.

A. one
B. two
C. three
D. four

17. Metal covers shall be of the same material of the box with which they are used or they shall be lined with a firmly attached insulating material that is NOT less than _____ thick, or they shall be listed for the purpose.

A. 1/32 in.
B. 1/8 in.
C. 1/16 in.
D. 3/32 in.

18. For electrical systems over 600 volts, where straight pulls of conductors in junction boxes are being made, the length of the box shall NOT be less than _____ the outside diameter of the largest shielded or lead-covered conductor or cable entering the box.

A. 8 times
B. 12 times
C. 31 times
D. 48 times

19. Handhole enclosure covers shall require the use of tools to open, or they shall weigh at LEAST over _____.

A. 25 lbs.
B. 50 lbs.
C. 75 lbs.
D. 100 lbs.

20. Outlet boxes used as the sole support of a ceiling-suspended (paddle) fan shall be listed, shall be marked as suitable for this purpose and shall not support ceiling-suspended (paddle) fans that weigh MORE than _____.

A. 70 lbs.
B. 50 lbs.
C. 35 lbs.
D. 25 lbs.

ARTICLE 320- ARMORED CABLE: TYPE AC
****

21. Type AC cable shall have an armor of flexible metal tape and shall have an internal bonding strip of _____ in contact with the armor its entire length.

  I. copper
  II. aluminum

A. I only
B. II only
C. either I or II
D. neither I nor II

22. When Type AC cable is installed in thermal insulation, the ampacity of the conductors shall be that of a _____ rated conductor.

A. 60° C
B. 75° C
C. 90° C
D. 90° F

23. Unless otherwise permitted, where installed on or across framing members, Type AC cable must be fastened at LEAST every _____.

A. 2 feet
B. 3 feet
C. 6 feet
D. 4½ feet

24. When installing AC cable, the bend radius of the curve of the inner edge of the bend shall NOT be less than _____ times the diameter of the cable.

A. four
B. five
C. seven
D. six

25. When AC cable is used to supply recessed luminaires in an accessible ceiling and the AC cable is unsupported, the cable shall have a MAXIMUM length of _____.

A. 10 feet
B. 4 feet
C. 6 feet
D. 4½ feet

26. Type AC cable shall be permitted for use _____.

A. for feeders
B. in wet locations
C. where exposed to physical damage
D. in damp locations

ARTICLE 324 - FLAT CONDUCTOR CABLE: TYPE FCC
****

27. When Type FCC cable is used for general-purpose multioutlet branch-circuit conductors, the ratings of the circuits shall NOT exceed _____.

A. 20 amperes
B. 30 amperes
C. 15 amperes
D. 50 amperes

28. Type FCC cable may be installed _____.

   I. under carpet squares
   II. on wall surfaces in surface metal raceways

A. I only
B. II only
C. neither I nor II
D. both I and II

29. Type FCC cable shall be listed and consist of a MAXIMUM of _____ conductors.

A. three
B. four
C. five
D. six

30. Type FCC systems are permitted to be used in _____.

A. office buildings
B. schools
C. houses
D. all of these

31. When Type FCC cable is installed floor-mounted under carpet squares, the carpet squares shall NOT be larger than _____ square.

A. 12 inches
B. 3 feet
C. 2 feet
D. 18 inches

32. For Type FCC systems, the voltage between ungrounded conductors shall NOT exceed _____.

A. 120 volts
B. 150 volts
C. 277 volts
D. 300 volts

ARTICLE 326 - INTEGRATED GAS SPACER CABLE: TYPE IGS
****

33. Type IGS cable shall NOT be used _____.

A. for underground installations
B. for service entrance conductors
C. as interior wiring
D. as branch-circuit conductors

34. The NEC® mandates the MINIMUM size conductor for Type IGS cable to be _____.

A. 2 AWG
B. 1/0 AWG
C. 4/0 AWG
D. 250 kcmil

35. Type IGS cable is rated for use at a MAXIMUM voltage of _____.

A. 6000 volts
B. 600 volts
C. 1000 volts
D. 2000 volts

36. The MAXIMUM allowable ampacity of size 500 kcmil Type IGS cable shall be _____.

A. 168 amperes
B. 380 amperes
C. 206 amperes
D. 320 amperes

ARTICLE 328 - MEDIUM VOLTAGE CABLE: TYPE MV
****

37. Type MV cable is a single or multiconductor solid dielectric insulated cable permitted for use on power systems rated up to and including _____.

A. 600 volts
B. 2000 volts
C. 2001 volts
D. 35,000 volts

38. Type MV cable is permitted to be used_____.

A. in messenger supported wiring
B. direct-buried
C. in cable trays
D. for all of these conditions

39. The ampacity of Type MV cable installed in cable tray shall be determined in accordance with _____ of the NEC®.

A. Section 310.60
B. Section 310.15(B)(16)
C. Section 392.80(B)
D. Section 313.92

ARTICLE 330 - METAL-CLAD CABLE: TYPE MC
****

40. The MINIMUM size copper or nickel-coated copper conductor permitted for Type MC cable is _____.

A. 12 AWG
B. 14 AWG
C. 16 AWG
D. 18 AWG

41. What is the MINIMUM bend radius for 1 inch diameter smooth sheath MC cable?

A. 7 inches
B. 10 inches
C. 12 inches
D. 15 inches

42. When Type MC cable is used as a "fixture-whip" to supply recessed luminaires within an accessible ceiling and the MC cable is unsupported, the cable shall have a MAXIMUM length of _____.

A. 10 feet
B. 4 feet
C. 4½ feet
D. 6 feet

43. Bends in corrugated sheath Type MC cable shall be made so that the radius of the curve of the inner edge of any bend shall NOT be less than _____ the external diameter of the metallic sheath.

A. 10 times
B. 7 times
C. 12 times
D. 15 times

44. Type MC cable is NOT permitted for use _____.

A. in cable trays
B. in any raceway
C. as aerial cable on a messenger
D. where exposed to chlorine vapors

45. Type MC cable containing three (3) size 12 AWG copper conductors shall be secured within at LEAST _____ of every outlet box, junction box, cabinet or panelboard.

A. 12 inches
B. 18 inches
C. 6 inches
D. 42 inches

ARTICLE 332 - MINERAL-INSULATED, METAL-SHEATHED CABLE: TYPE MI

46. In general, Type MI cable shall be supported and secured by straps, staples or similar fittings designed and installed so as not to damage the cable, at intervals NOT exceeding _____.

A. 6 feet
B. 4½ feet
C. 4 feet
D. 5 feet

47. Where the outer sheath of Type MI cable is made of _____, an equipment grounding conductor shall be provided.

    I. steel
    II. copper

A. I only
B. II only
C. neither I nor II
D. both I and II

48. Where trade size 3/4 inch Type MI cable is installed in Class II, Division 2 locations, the radius of the inner edge of the bend shall NOT be less than _____ times the external diameter.

A. three
B. four
C. five
D. ten

49. Disregarding all exceptions, which one of the following statements about Type MI cable is correct?

A. It may be used in hazardous (classified) locations.
B. It shall not be used where exposed to oil and gasoline.
C. It shall not be used for services.
D. It shall not be used where concealed.

50. Type MI cable conductors shall be of _____ with a resistance corresponding to standard AWG and kcmil sizes.

A. stranded copper only
B. solid copper, nickel, or nickel-coated copper
C. stranded or solid aluminum or copper
D. stranded or solid copper

END OF UNIT SIX

UNIT SEVEN

NEC® QUESTIONS FROM ARTICLE 334 THROUGH ARTICLE 356

The following National Electrical Code® questions are typical of questions encountered on all electricians' exams, based on the above referenced Articles of the Code. Select the best answer from the choices given then review your answers with the answer key at the back of this book.

ARTICLE 334 - NONMETALLIC-SHEATHED CABLE: TYPES NM, NMC and NMS
****

1. Type NM cable shall NOT be permitted to be used _____.

    I. in cable trays
    II. as service-entrance conductors

A. I only
B. II only
C. neither I nor II
D. both I and II

2. Insulated conductors shall be rated at _____ in type NM-B cable.

A. 60 deg. C
B. 75 deg. C
C. 90 deg. C
D. 90 deg. F

3. The largest size copper conductor permitted for nonmetallic sheathed cable is _____.

A. 4 AWG
B. 2 AWG
C. 1 AWG
D. 1/0 AWG

4. Where NMC cable is run at angles with joists in unfinished basements, it shall be permissible to secure cables NOT smaller than size _____ directly to the lower edges of the joist.

A. 12/2 AWG
B. 10/2 AWG
C. 10/3 AWG
D. 8/3 AWG

5. Where exposed Type NM cable passes through a floor, the cable shall be protected from physical damage by an approved means extending at LEAST _____ above the floor.

A. 4 inches
B. 6 inches
C. 8 inches
D. 10 inches

6. Disregarding exceptions, Type NM cable shall be secured in place at intervals NOT exceeding _____ and within 12 inches of every box or loadcenter.

A. 3 feet
B. 4½ feet
C. 4 feet
D. 6 feet

7. The ampacity of Type NM cable shall be that of _____ conductors.

A. 60 deg. F
B. 90 deg. C
C. 75 deg. C
D. 60 deg. C

8. Which of the following listed cables have an overall covering that is fungus resistant?

A. Type NM
B. Type NMS
C. Type NMC
D. Type MI

9. Type NM cable is NOT permitted for use _____.

A. in wet locations
B. in Type V construction
C. for exposed work in dry locations
D. in any of the above listed installations

ARTICLE 338 - SERVICE ENTRANCE CABLE: TYPES SE and USE
****

10. Type SE cable can be used for interior work when which of the following conditions is met?

A. The conductors are of the thermoset or thermoplastic type.
B. The circuit is protected by a circuit breaker rated not more than 20 amperes.
C. The circuit is GFCI protected.
D. The circuit is AFCI protected.

11. Bends in SE cable shall be made so that the radius of the curve of the inner edge of any bend shall not be LESS than:

A. five times the diameter of the cable.
B. five inches minimum.
C. seven times the circular mil area of the conductors.
D. six inches minimum.

12. Underground service-entrance cable (USE) shall NOT be used under which of the following listed conditions?

A. Enclosed in PVC conduit.
B. In wet locations.
C. For interior wiring.
D. Where one conductor is uninsulated.

ARTICLE 340 - UNDERGROUND FEEDER and BRANCH CIRCUIT CABLE: TYPE UF
****

13. The ampacity of UF cable shall be that of _____ conductors.

A. 60° C
B. 75° C
C. 90° C
D. 80° C

14. The largest size conductor permitted for Type UF cable is _____.

A. 4 AWG
B. 2/0 AWG
C. 4/0 AWG
D. 2 AWG

15. Is Type UF cable permitted to be installed underground as a single conductor?

A. No, not under any circumstances.
B. Yes, if enclosed in a nonmetallic raceway.
C. No, unless all the conductors of the same circuit are in separate trenches.
D. Yes, where all the conductors of the same circuit are contained within the same trench.

16. Type UF cable is permitted to be used _____.

A. as service-entrance cables
B. in storage battery rooms
C. in motion picture studios
D. for interior wiring in houses

17. Type UF cable is permitted to have _____ bare equipment grounding conductor(s).

A. no
B. one
C. two
D. three

ARTICLE 342 - INTERMEDIATE METAL CONDUIT: TYPE IMC

18. When IMC is threaded in the field, a standard cutting die with a ____ taper per ft. shall be used.

A. 3/8 in.
B. 1/2 in.
C. 3/4 in.
D. 1 in.

19. In general, IMC shall be supported at intervals NOT exceeding _____ .

A. 3 feet
B. 4½ feet
C. 6 feet
D. 10 feet

20. The NEC® mandates the largest standard trade size of IMC to be _____ .

A. 1 inch
B. 4 inches
C. 5 inches
D. 6 inches

21. Where threadless couplings and connectors are used with IMC buried in concrete, the fittings shall be of the _____ type.

A. raintight
B. watertight
C. compression
D. concretetight

22. Exposed vertical risers of threaded IMC from industrial machinery or fixed equipment shall be permitted to be supported at intervals of NOT exceeding _____, where the conduit is supported and securely fastened at the top and bottom of the riser.

A. 8 feet
B. 10 feet
C. 20 feet
D. 30 feet

ARTICLE 344 - RIGID METAL CONDUIT: TYPE RMC
****

23. Where a full shoe type conduit bender is used for a field bend of trade size 2 inch rigid metal conduit (RMC), what is the MINIMUM radius of the curve of the bend to the centerline of the conduit as permitted by the NEC®?

A. 9½ inches
B. 12 inches
C. 10½ inches
D. 8¼ inches

24. The NEC® mandates the MAXIMUM distance between supports for standard trade size 4 in. rigid metal conduit (RMC) with threaded couplings to be_____.

A. 6 feet
B. 10 feet
C. 16 feet
D. 20 feet

25. For enclosing service-entrance conductors, rigid metal conduit (RMC) larger than standard trade size _____ shall NOT be used.

A. 2 in.
B. 4 in.
C. 5 in.
D. 6 in.

26. Which of the following statements, if any, about rigid metal conduit (RMC) is/are true?

    I. Steel locknuts and bushings shall be permitted to be used with aluminum rigid metal conduit.
    II. RMC shall be permitted as an equipment grounding conductor.

A. I only
B. II only
C. both I and II
D. neither I nor II

27. Where a run of trade size 3/4 in. RMC is mounted horizontally on a flat concrete wall, what is the MAXIMUM allowable distance from each outlet box or panelboard that the conduit must be securely fastened?

A. 2 feet
B. 3 feet
C. 4 feet
D. 5 feet

28. Where threadless couplings and connectors are used with RMC installed in wet locations, the fittings shall be _____.

A. weatherproof type
B. watertight type
C. listed for use in wet locations
D. prohibited

ARTICLE 348 - FLEXIBLE METAL CONDUIT: TYPE FMC
****

29. Disregarding exceptions, flexible metal conduit (FMC) shall be supported at LEAST every _____ and within 12 inches of an outlet box or panelboard.

A. 4½ feet
B. 6 feet
C. 4 feet
D. 8 feet

30. The NEC® permits trade size 3/8 in. flexible metal conduit (FMC) to be used for tap connections to luminaires if the FMC length does NOT exceed _____.

A. 18 inches
B. 6 feet
C. 4 feet
D. 10 feet

31. The NEC® mandates the largest trade size of flexible metal conduit (FMC) to be used is _____.

A. 1 in.
B. 2 in.
C. 3/4 in.
D. 4 in.

32. FMC is permitted to be used in wet locations _____.

A. where the conductors contained in the FMC are listed for use in wet locations
B. where the conductors contained in the FMC have a 90° C temperature rating
C. where the FMC has a maximum length of 4 feet
D. never

33. Where not counting the equipment grounding conductors, the MAXIMUM number of size 12 AWG THWN conductors permitted in a standard trade size 3/8 in. flexible metal conduit (FMC) is _____.

A. one
B. two
C. three
D. four

34. When installing flexible metal conduit (FMC), which one of the following listed connectors is NOT permitted to be used for concealed raceway installations?

A. angle type
B. screw-in type
C. set-screw type
D. clamp-on type

ARTICLE 350 - LIQUIDTIGHT FLEXIBLE METAL CONDUIT: TYPE LFMC
****

35. LFMC is permitted to have not more than the equivalent of _____ 90 deg. bend(s) between pull points or outlet boxes.

A. one
B. two
C. three
D. four

36. Where liquidtight flexible metal conduit (LFMC) is used to connect to motors and flexibility is required, a/an _____ conductor must be installed.

A. grounded
B. bonding
C. equipment grounding
D. equipment grounded

37. Disregarding exceptions, liquidtight flexible metal conduit (LFMC) smaller than electrical trade size _____ shall NOT be used.

A. 3/8 in.
B. 1/2 in.
C. 3/4 in.
D. 1 in.

38. In general, liquidtight flexible metal conduit (LFMC) shall be securely fastened in place WITHIN _____ of each box or other conduit termination and shall be supported and secured at intervals NOT to exceed _____.

A. 12 in. - 4½ ft.
B. 12 in. - 6 ft.
C. 18 in. - 4½ ft.
D. 24 in. - 4½ ft.

ARTICLE 352 – RIGID POLYVINYL CHLORIDE CONDUIT: TYPE PVC
****

39. Rigid polyvinyl chloride (PVC) conduit shall NOT be used _____.

   I. for the support of lighting fixtures
   II. where subject to physical damage, unless identified for such use

A. I only
B. II only
C. neither I nor II
D. both I and II

40. The NEC® mandates the MAXIMUM distance between supports for standard trade size 2 in. Schedule 40 rigid polyvinyl chloride (PVC) conduit to be _____.

A. 3 feet
B. 10 feet
C. 6 feet
D. 5 feet

41. Rigid PVC conduit shall be securely fastened within at LEAST _____ of an outlet box, junction box or panelboard.

A. 1 foot
B. 2 feet
C. 2½ feet
D. 3 feet

42. In an underground installed rigid polyvinyl chloride (PVC) conduit system that consist of 20 feet in length between pulling points, what is the MAXIMUM number of bends that this run may have?

A. 4 – 90 deg.
B. 6 – 90 deg.
C. 4 – 120 deg.
D. 2 – 360 deg.

43. Unless listed otherwise, rigid PVC conduit is not permitted to be installed where subject to ambient temperatures in EXCESS of _____.

A. 50° C
B. 122° C
C. 90° C
D. 100° C

44. What expected change in length, due to expansion, is 100 ft. of rigid PVC conduit to have, when the PVC is installed outdoors and is exposed to a 75 deg. F temperature change from the coldest day to the warmest day in a calendar year?

A. 3.40 in.
B. 3.04 in.
C. 4.03 in.
D. 2.84 in.

45. Rigid PVC conduit larger than trade size _____ shall NOT be used.

A. 2 in.
B. 3 in.
C. 4 in.
D. 6 in.

ARTICLE 356 - LIQUIDTIGHT FLEXIBLE NONMETALLIC CONDUIT: TYPE LFNC

****

46. Standard trade size 3/8 in. liquidtight flexible nonmetallic conduit (LFNC) is permitted for _____.

   I. enclosing the leads of motors
   II. for tap connections to luminaires

A. I only
B. II only
C. neither I nor II
D. both I and II

47. Horizontal runs of LFNC supported by openings through framing members at intervals NOT exceeding _____ and securely fastened WITHIN _____ of termination points shall be permitted.

A. 4½ ft. – 18 in.
B. 3 ft. – 12 in.
C. 3 ft. – 18 in.
D. 6 ft. – 18 in.

48. In compliance with the NEC®, LFNC shall NOT be used _____.

A. for encasement in concrete
B. for outdoor locations
C. where subject to physical damage
D. for all the above listed conditions

49. The NEC® mandates LFNC larger than trade size _____ shall not be used.

A. 3/4 in.
B. 1 in.
C. 2 in.
D. 4 in.

50. For 1 in. trade size LFNC, the radius of the curve to the centerline of the bend shall NOT be less than _____.

A. 4 inches
B. 5 inches
C. 6 inches
D. 8 inches

END OF UNIT SEVEN

****

UNIT EIGHT

NEC® QUESTIONS FROM ARTICLE 358 THROUGH ARTICLE 388

The following National Electrical Code® questions are typical of questions encountered on all electricians' exams, based on the above referenced Articles of the Code. Select the best answer from the choices given then review your answers with the answer key at the back of this book.

ARTICLE 358 - ELECTRICAL METALLIC TUBING: TYPE EMT
****

1. Where buried in masonry, the fittings of EMT shall be of the _____ type.

A. concretetight
B. watertight
C. compression
D. weatherproof

2. Electrical metallic tubing (EMT) is permitted to be _____.

   I. threaded on the jobsite
   II. factory threaded

A. I only
B. II only
C. neither I nor II
D. both I and II

3. To enclose service-entrance conductors, EMT larger than standard trade size ____ shall NOT be used.

A. 1 in.
B. 2 in.
C. 4 in.
D. 6 in.

4. For field bends of EMT made with a bending machine, the MINIMUM radius of the bend shall NOT be less than as indicated in _____ of the NEC®.

A. Table 9, Chpt. 2
B. Table 4, Chpt. 9
C. Table 2, Chpt. 9
D. Table 4, Chpt. 2

5. Disregarding exceptions, when installing EMT the run of tubing shall be securely fastened at LEAST every _____.

A. 6 feet
B. 10 feet
C. 8 feet
D. 5 feet

6. Horizontal runs of EMT supported by openings through framing members shall be securely fastened WITHIN _____ of each outlet box, junction box, or device box.

A. 12 inches
B. 10 feet
C. 24 inches
D. 3 feet

ARTICLE 360 - FLEXIBLE METALLIC TUBING: TYPE FMT
****

7. The MAXIMUM trade size flexible metallic tubing (FMT) permitted is _____.

A. 1 in.
B. 2 in.
C. 4 in.
D. 3/4 in.

8. Flexible metallic tubing (FMT) shall NOT be used in lengths over _____.

A. 6 feet
B. 8 feet
C. 10 feet
D. 4½ feet

ARTICLE 362 - ELECTRICAL NONMETALLIC TUBING: TYPE ENT
****

9. Current-carrying conductors installed within electrical nonmetallic tubing (ENT) may carry a MAXIMUM of _____.

A. 300 volts
B. 277 volts
C. 480 volts
D. 600 volts

10. The NEC® mandates ENT larger than _____ trade size shall not be used.

A. 3/4 in.
B. 2 in.
C. 1 in.
D. 4 in.

11. Unless listed otherwise, ENT is not permitted to be installed in areas where subject to ambient temperatures in excess of _____.

A. 100° F
B. 150° F
C. 122° F
D. 90° F

12. Where _____ is installed, ENT is permitted to be used within walls and ceilings in buildings exceeding three (3) floors above grade.

A. GFCI protection
B. AFCI protection
C. a fire sprinkler system
D. an equipment grounding conductor

ARTICLE 366 - AUXILIARY GUTTERS
****

13. Nonmetallic auxiliary gutters shall be supported at intervals NOT exceeding _____ and at each end or joint, unless listed for other support intervals.

A. 3 feet
B. 4 feet
C. 5 feet
D. 6 feet

14. What is the ampacity derating factor to be applied to current-carrying conductors when a sheet metal auxiliary gutter contains 34 current-carrying conductors?

A. 49 percent
B. 53 percent
C. 40 percent
D. 55 percent

15. What percent of an auxiliary gutter area may be occupied by splices, taps, and conductors at any point?

A. 20 percent
B. 30 percent
C. 40 percent
D. 75 percent

16. Disregarding exceptions, auxiliary gutters shall NOT extend more than _____ beyond the equipment they supplement.

A. 6 feet
B. 30 inches
C. 10 feet
D. 30 feet

17. Current-carrying metal parts installed in an auxiliary gutter shall be securely supported so that the MINIMUM clearance to any metal surface of the auxiliary gutter is NOT less than ____.

A. 1 in.
B. 2 in.
C. 3/4 in.
D. 2½ in.

18. When the conductor derating factors of Section 310.15(B)(3)(a) of the NEC® are applied, sheet metal auxiliary gutters shall NOT contain more than _____ conductors at any cross-section.

A. 20
B. 25
C. 30
D. none of these

ARTICLE 368 - BUSWAYS
****

19. Busways shall be securely supported at intervals NOT exceeding _____ unless otherwise designed and marked.

A. 6 feet
B. 5 feet
C. 10 feet
D. 12 feet

20. In an industrial establishment, what is the MAXIMUM length of 200 ampere rated busway that may be tapped to a 600 ampere rated busway, without additional overcurrent protection?

A. 10 feet
B. 25 feet
C. 50 feet
D. 75 feet

21. Which of the following statement(s), if any, is/are true regarding busways?

    I. Busway is not required to be grounded.
    II. A dead end of a busway shall be open.

A. I only
B. II only
C. both I and II
D. neither I nor II

22. Which of the following statements regarding busways is/are true? Busways shall NOT be installed:

A. where subject to severe physical damage.
B. outdoors or in wet locations unless identified for such use.
C. in hoistways.
D. All of these statements are true.

ARTICLE 370 - CABLEBUS
****

23. The MINIMUM size of conductors permitted in a cablebus is _____.

A. 1 AWG
B. 1/0 AWG
C. 2 AWG
D. 2/0 AWG

24. The current-carrying conductors of cablebus shall have an insulation rating of at LEAST _____ or higher.

A. 75 deg. F
B. 167 deg. C
C. 60 deg. F
D. 75 deg. C

25. Disregarding exceptions, cablebus shall be securely supported at intervals NOT exceeding _____.

A. 6 feet
B. 10 feet
C. 12 feet
D. 8 feet

ARTICLE 376 - METAL WIREWAYS
****

26. What is the MAXIMUM number of current-carrying conductors the NEC® permits in a metal wireway without derating the ampacity of the conductors?

A. 20
B. 3
C. 30
D. 42

27. Metal wireways, where run vertically, shall be supported at intervals NOT to exceed _____.

A. 5 feet
B. 10 feet
C. 15 feet
D. 4½ feet

28. In general, the cross-sectional area of the conductors contained in a metal wireway shall NOT exceed _____ of the interior cross-sectional area of the wireway.

A. 30 percent
B. 20 percent
C. 40 percent
D. 75 percent

29. When a metal wireway contains splices and taps, the conductors, splices, and taps, shall NOT fill the wireway to more than _____ of its area at that point.

A. 20 percent
B. 30 percent
C. 40 percent
D. 75 percent

ARTICLE 378 - NONMETALLIC WIREWAYS
****

30. Nonmetallic wireways shall be supported where run horizontally at intervals NOT to exceed _____ and at each end or joint, unless listed for other support intervals.

A. 3 feet
B. 4 feet
C. 10 feet
D. 15 feet

31. Expansion fittings for nonmetallic wireways shall be provided to compensate for:

A. the weight of the conductors contained within the wireway.
B. the thermal expansion and contraction of the wireway.
C. the heat differential of the conductors contained in the wireway.
D. the temperature ratio of the conduit connected to the wireway and the nonmetallic wireway.

32. Where insulated conductors of 4 AWG or larger are pulled through a nonmetallic wireway, the distance between raceway and cable entries enclosing the same conductor shall NOT be less than _____ times the trade size of the raceway, where angle pulls are to be made.

A. four
B. eight
C. two
D. six

33. Nonmetallic wireways are permitted to be installed _____.

   I. where subject to corrosive environments
   II. in all hazardous (classified) locations

A. I only
B. II only
C. neither I nor II
D. both I and II

34. Where a nonmetallic wireway does not contain splices and taps, the sum of cross-sectional areas of all contained conductors at any cross section of the nonmetallic wireway shall NOT exceed _____ of the interior cross-sectional area of the wireway.

A. 30 percent
B. 75 percent
C. 20 percent
D. 40 percent

ARTICLE 382 - NONMETALLIC EXTENSIONS
****

35. Concealable nonmetallic extensions shall be clearly and durably marked on both sides at intervals of NOT more than _____, indentifying the material of conductors, maximum temperature rating and ampacity.

A. 24 inches
B. 18 inches
C. 36 inches
D. 42 inches

36. Exposed nonmetallic surface extensions shall be permitted to be run in any direction from an existing outlet, but NOT within _____ from the floor.

A. 1 foot
B. 1½ feet
C. 2 feet
D. 2 inches

37. Nonmetallic surface extensions shall be secured in place by approved means at intervals NOT exceeding _____.

A. 20 inches
B. 18 inches
C. 8 inches
D. 4½ feet

38. The voltage between conductors for nonmetallic surface extensions shall NOT exceed _____.

A. 120 volts
B. 150 volts
C. 300 volts
D. 250 volts

ARTICLE 384 - STRUT-TYPE CHANNEL RACEWAY
****

39. Unbroken lengths of strut-type channel raceways containing conductors are permitted to be used _____.

   I. above a lift-out type ceiling, if accessible
   II. through walls

A. I only
B. II only
C. neither I nor II
D. both I and II

40. Where suspension mounted in air, strut-type channel raceways shall be secured at intervals NOT to exceed _____.

A. 4½ feet
B. 6 feet
C. 8 feet
D. 10 feet

41. Strut-type channel raceways are permitted to be constructed of _____ materials.

   I. nonmetallic
   II. metallic

A. I only
B. II only
C. either I or II
D. both I and II

ARTICLE 386 - SURFACE METAL RACEWAYS
****

42. It is not necessary to derate the ampacity of conductors installed in surface metal raceways if the number of current-carrying conductors does NOT exceed_____.

A. 3
B. 20
C. 6
D. 30

43. It is permissible to run unbroken lengths of surface metal raceways through _____.

   I. dry walls
   II. floors subject to water

A. I only
B. II only
C. neither I nor II
D. both I and II

44. When a transition is made from EMT to a surface metal raceway, a _____ shall be provided.

A. bushing
B. insulating bushing
C. means for connecting an equipment grounding conductor
D. none of the above

45. The NEC® mandates surface metal raceways are not permitted to be used where the voltage is _____ or more between the conductors, unless the surface metal raceway has a thickness of not less than 0.040 in.

A. 150 volts
B. 300 volts
C. 277 volts
D. 240 volts

ARTICLE 388 - SURFACE NONMETALLIC RACEWAYS
****

46. Unless listed for a higher voltage, surface nonmetallic raceways shall not be used when the voltage between the conductors EXCEEDS _____.

A. 150 volts
B. 277 volts
C. 300 volts
D. 600 volts

47. When a surface nonmetallic raceway contains splices and taps, the raceway is permitted to be filled to NO more than _____ of its area at that point.

A. 60 percent
B. 75 percent
C. 30 percent
D. 20 percent

48. Surface nonmetallic raceways shall be securely supported at intervals NOT to exceed _____.

A. 3 feet
B. 6 feet
C. 10 feet
D. the manufacturer's instructions

49. When combination surface nonmetallic raceways are used both for signaling and for lighting and power circuits the _____.

A. insulated power conductors shall be red in color
B. signaling conductors shall have an insulation rating equal to the power conductors
C. different systems shall be run in separate compartments
D. conductors shall be stranded copper

50. Splices and taps in surface nonmetallic raceways without covers capable of being opened in place shall be _____.

A. permitted anywhere within the raceway
B. made only in boxes
C. made only in raceway lengths exceeding 12 inches
D. made only with conductors having a temperature rating of not less than 90° C

END OF UNIT EIGHT
****

UNIT NINE

NEC® QUESTIONS FROM ARTICLE 390 THROUGH ARTICLE 406

The following National Electrical Code® questions are typical of questions encountered on all electricians' exams, based on the above referenced Articles of the Code. Select the best answer from the choices given then review your answers with the answer key at the back of this book.

ARTICLE 390 – UNDERFLOOR RACEWAYS
****

1. In general, 4 inch wide underfloor raceways shall have a covering of wood or concrete of NOT less than _____ above the raceway.

A. ½ in.
B. ¾ in.
C. 1 in.
D. 1 ¼ in.

2. Where a receptacle outlet is removed from an underfloor raceway, the conductors supplying the outlet _____.

A. shall be capped with an approved insulating material
B. shall be taped off with red colored tape
C. are permitted to be marked, identified and remain in the raceway
D. shall be removed from the raceway

ARTICLE 392 - CABLE TRAYS
****

3. For industrial establishments, when installed in cable trays, single conductors used as equipment grounding conductors shall be at LEAST size _____ or larger.

A. 1/0 AWG
B. 4/0 AWG
C. 4 AWG
D. 6 AWG

4. What is the MAXIMUM rung spacing for ladder type cable trays containing single conductors sized at 1/0 AWG through 4/0 AWG?

A. 15 inches
B. 12 inches
C. 6 inches
D. 9 inches

5. Steel cable trays shall not be used as equipment grounding conductors for circuits with ground-fault protection above _____.

A. 200 amperes
B. 300 amperes
C. 600 amperes
D. 800 amperes

6. Under which of the following conditions, if any, is a steel cable tray permitted to be used as a grounding conductor?

   I. The cable tray sections shall be legibly marked to show the cross-sectional area of the metal.
   II. The cable tray sections must be identified for grounding purposes.

A. I only
B. II only
C. neither I nor II
D. both I and II

7. The NEC® states cable trays shall NOT be used _____.

A. in hoistways
B. in basements
C. outdoors
D. in any of these locations

8. Where solid bottom cable trays contain multiconductor cables of 4/0 AWG or larger, the sum of the diameters of all cables shall NOT exceed _____ of the cable tray width, and the cables shall be installed in a single layer.

A. 90 percent
B. 80 percent
C. 70 percent
D. 60 percent

9. Cables over 600 volts and those rated 600 volts or less, are permitted to be installed in a common cable tray without a fixed barrier, where the cables OVER 600 volts are _____.

A. Type MI
B. Type MC
C. Type AC
D. Type NM

10. Where single conductors with THWN insulation are installed in a single layer in uncovered cable trays, with a maintained space of not less than one cable diameter between individual conductors, the ampacity of 1/0 AWG and larger cables shall not exceed the allowable ampacities in _____ of the NEC®.

A. Table 310.15(B)(16)
B. Table 310.15(B)(17)
C. Table 310.15(B)(15)
D. Table 310.15(B)(19)

11. Cable splices are permitted in a cable tray, provided _____.

A. they are accessible
B. the splices are contained in a junction box
C. the conductors are size 1/0 AWG or larger
D. the splices are made with compression type fittings

12. Where size 4/0 AWG multiconductor cables, rated 2,000 volts or less, are installed in a ladder type cable tray, what is the MAXIMUM allowable fill area, in square inches, of a 9 inch wide cable tray?

A. 9 sq. in.
B. 10 ½ sq. in.
C. 12 sq. in.
D. 14 sq. in.

ARTICLE 394 - CONCEALED KNOB-and-TUBE WIRING
****

13. Knob-and-tube wiring shall be supported within 6 inches of each side of each tap or splice and at intervals NOT exceeding _____.

A. 2½ feet
B. 3 feet
C. 6 feet
D. 4½ feet

14. Splices and taps for knob-and-tube wiring shall _____ unless approved splicing devices are used; in-line splices shall not be used.

A. be soldered
B. be wrapped with friction tape
C. not be soldered
D. be completed with split-bolt connections

15. A MINIMUM clearance of NOT less than _____ shall be maintained between knob-and-tube wiring and metallic water lines.

A. 1 inch
B. 3 inches
C. 2 inches
D. 4 inches

16. Where knob-and-tube conductors pass through cross members in plastered walls, the conductors shall be protected by insulating tubes extending NOT less than _____ beyond the wood member.

A. 1 inch
B. 2 inches
C. 3 inches
D. 4 inches

ARTICLE 396 – MESSENGER-SUPPORTED WIRING
****

17. Which of the following listed wiring methods shall be permitted to be installed in messenger-supported wiring systems?

A. Multiconductor service-entrance cable
B. Type MI cable
C. Multiconductor underground feeder cable
D. All of these

18. Messenger-supported wiring is an exposed wiring method that uses a messenger wire to support _____ conductors.

   I. bare
   II. insulated

A. I only
B. II only
C. either I or II
D. both I and II

19. Messenger-supported conductors shall NOT be permitted to come into contact with the _____.

   I. messenger supports
   II. structural members

A. I only
B. II only
C. neither I nor II
D. both I and II

20. Where messenger-supported conductors are exposed to weather, the conductors shall be listed for use in _____ locations.

A. wet
B. damp
C. hazardous
D. high moisture

ARTICLE 398 - OPEN WIRING ON INSULATORS
****

21. Open wiring on insulators shall be permitted on systems of _____ or less.

A. 250 volts
B. 480 volts
C. 600 volts
D. All of the above

22. When open wiring on insulators is installed WITHIN _____ of the floor, it shall be protected from physical damage.

A. 12 feet
B. 10 feet
C. 8 feet
D. 7 feet

23. Where nails are used to mount knobs for the support of open wiring on insulators, they shall NOT be smaller than _____ penny.

A. ten
B. six
C. eight
D. sixteen

ARTICLE 400 - FLEXIBLE CORDS and CABLES
****

24. A type of cable that may be used for elevator lighting is Type _____.

A. HPD
B. SEL
C. SJEO
D. EO

25. The MAXIMUM allowable ampacity of size 14/2 AWG Type SJT cord is _____.

A. 15 amperes
B. 13 amperes
C. 20 amperes
D. 18 amperes

26. Flexible cords and cables shall NOT be used _____.

A. for connection of portable signs
B. where run through holes in walls
C. for connection to stationary appliances
D. for wiring of luminaires

27. In general, a flexible cord permitted to be used in show windows and show cases is Type _____.

A. SVT
B. SVTO
C. SJE
D. SWO

28. The MINIMUM size copper multiconductor portable cable permitted to be used to connect mobile equipment and machinery over 600 volts is _____ and shall employ flexible stranding.

A. 12 AWG
B. 10 AWG
C. 14 AWG
D. 8 AWG

29. Where conductors within a cord are on a 4-wire, 3-phase, wye circuit where the major portion of the load consist of nonlinear loads, such as fluorescent lighting, the neutral shall be considered to be a _____.

A. equipment grounding conductor
B. current-carrying conductor
C. noncurrent-carrying conductor
D. ungrounded conductor

30. In a flexible cord the grounded conductor insulation shall be _____ in color.

A. green
B. red or black
C. white or gray
D. green or black

ARTICLE 402 - FIXTURE WIRES
****

31. Fixture wires shall NOT be smaller than size _____.

A. 16 AWG
B. 14 AWG
C. 18 AWG
D. 20 AWG

32. The MAXIMUM allowable ampacity of size 16 AWG TFN fixture wire is _____.

A. 6 amperes
B. 8 amperes
C. 17 amperes
D. 10 amperes

33. The MAXIMUM operating temperature of Type PFF fixture wire is _____ .

A. 302° F
B. 150° F
C. 392° F
D. 90° C

34. Type TFFN fixture wire has_____ insulation.

A. thermo-silicone
B. cross-linked polyolefin
C. thermonylon
D. thermoplastic

35. The MAXIMUM operating temperature for thermoplastic covered solid fixture wire is _____.

A. 60° F
B. 75° F
C. 90° C
D. 140° F

ARTICLE 404 - SWITCHES
****

36. In general, the MAXIMUM height above the floor of the operating handle of a standard disconnect switch, when it is in the ON position, must NOT exceed _____.

A. 5½ ft.
B. 6 ft.
C. 6½ ft.
D. 6 ft., 7 in.

37. Where a knife switch is rated at 700 amperes and used for isolating a load, at which one of the following listed voltages may the switch be operated?

A. 120 volts
B. 460 volts
C. 208 volts
D. 1200 volts

38. Where a two-gang box contains two (2) single-pole switches, unless the box is equipped with permanently installed barriers, the voltage between the adjacent switches shall NOT be in excess of _____.

A. 120 volts
B. 300 volts
C. 480 volts
D. 240 volts

38. Three-way and four-way switches shall be wired so that all switching is done _____.

A. only in the ungrounded circuit conductor
B. only in the grounded circuit conductor
C. either in the grounded or ungrounded circuit conductor
D. only in the white circuit conductor

40. When an ac general-use snap switch is used for control of motor loads, the load shall NOT exceed _____ of the ampere rating of the switch at its rated voltage.

A. 50 percent
B. 75 percent
C. 80 percent
D. 100 percent

41. When aluminum conductors are connected to snap switches rated 20 amperes or less, the switches must be listed and MARKED _____.

A. AL/CU
B. AL/CO
C. CO/ALR
D. AL/COR

42. Unless listed for the control of other loads and installed accordingly, general-use dimmer switches shall be used ONLY to control _____.

A. ceiling fans
B. permanently installed incandescent luminaires
C. permanently installed fluorescent luminaires
D. temporarily or permanently installed incandescent or fluorescent luminaires

ARTICLE 406 - RECEPTACLES, CORD CONNECTORS, and ATTACHMENT PLUGS (CAPS)
****

43. A receptacle installed within a bathtub or shower space _____.

A. shall be GFCI protected
B. shall be on a dedicated branch circuit
C. shall be weatherproof
D. is prohibited

44. Which of the following methods is an acceptable marking for the termination of the grounding conductor on a grounding type receptacle?

A. A green colored hexagonal-headed or shaped terminal screw.
B. An orange dot.
C. A white colored round headed screw.
D. An orange colored hexagonal screw.

45. Receptacles with a 15 ampere rating and designed to be directly connected to aluminum conductors shall be MARKED _____.

A. CU/ALR
B. AL/CRU
C. CO/ALR
D. CU/ALU

46. Receptacles installed in countertops shall NOT be installed _____.

A. in the horizontal position
B. in a face-up position
C. flush with the counter-top surface
D. in a vertical position

47. Receptacles incorporating an isolated grounding conductor connection intended for the reduction of electrical noise, shall be identified by _____ located on the face of the receptacle.

A. an orange triangle
B. a green triangle
C. an orange dot
D. a yellow happy face

48. Where a straight-blade, 15- or 20-ampere, 125 volt, receptacle is installed in a wet location, the receptacle enclosure must be listed as _____ whether or not the attachment cap is inserted.

A. weatherproof
B. raintight
C. watertight
D. weather-resistant

49. All 15- and 20-ampere, 125 and 250 volt, nonlocking receptacles located in wet locations shall be listed _____ type.

A. weatherproof
B. waterproof
C. weather-resistant
D. water-resistant

50. A non-grounding-type receptacle shall be permitted to be replaced with a grounding-type receptacle _____.

A. never
B. where supplied through an arc-fault circuit interrupter
C. where the grounded conductor is connected to the grounding terminal on the device
D. where supplied through a ground-fault circuit interrupter

END OF UNIT NINE

UNIT TEN

NEC® QUESTIONS FROM ARTICLE 408 THROUGH ARTICLE 426

The following National Electrical Code® questions are typical of questions encountered on all electricians' exams, based on the above referenced Articles of the Code. Select the best answer from the choices given then review your answers with the answer key at the back of this book.

ARTICLE 408 - SWITCHBOARDS and PANELBOARDS
****

1. Disregarding exceptions, when a switchboard or panelboard is supplied from a 3-phase, 4-wire delta-connected system, _____ shall be the phase having the higher voltage to ground.

A. the A phase
B. the B phase
C. the C phase
D. any phase

2. Panelboards equipped with snap switches (circuit breakers) rated at 30 amperes or less shall have overcurrent protection NOT in excess of _____.

A. 200 amperes
B. 225 amperes
C. 100 amperes
D. 400 amperes

3. As a general rule, all panelboards are required to have overcurrent protection. An EXCEPTION to this rule is _____.

A. panelboards that supply a second bus structure within the same panelboard assembly
B. for existing panelboards in a one-family dwelling used as service equipment
C. panelboards containing less than 42 overcurrent devices
D. panelboards containing only single-pole overcurrent devices

4. What is the MAXIMUM length a conduit may rise above the bottom of a floor-standing switchboard or panelboard?

A. 10 inches
B. 8 inches
C. 3 inches
D. No more than the diameter of the raceway.

5. As viewed from the front of a 3-phase open panelboard or switchboard, the *"A"* phase shall be the _____.

A. phase on the left
B. phase in the center
C. phase on the right
D. phase on the left, right or center

6. What is the MINIMUM distance permitted between the bottom of a switchboard and the noninsulated busbars housed in the switchboard?

A. 10 inches
B. 8 inches
C. 6 inches
D. 4 inches

7. In general, if a switchboard is used as service equipment, it shall be provided with a main bonding jumper within the switchboard for connecting the grounded service conductor on its _____ side to the switchboard frame.

    I. load
    II. supply

A. I only
B. II only
C. either I or II
D. neither I nor II

8. An insulated conductor used within a switchboard shall _____.

   I. be flame retardant
   II. have a voltage rating equal to the busbars in the switchboard

A. I only
B. II only
C. neither nor II
D. both I and II

9. Metallic surface-type panelboards installed in damp or wet locations shall be mounted so there is at LEAST _____ air space between the wall or other supporting surface.

A. 1/8 in.
B. 1/4 in.
C. 3/8 in.
D. 1/2 in.

10. In compliance with the NEC®, the MINIMUM allowable headroom for workspace about panelboards and switchboards used as service equipment in a commercial building is _____.

A. 6 ½ feet
B. 7 feet
C. 6 feet
D. 8 feet

11. A split-bus panelboard installed in a dwelling unit shall NOT contain more than _____ branch-circuit breakers.

A. 30
B. 36
C. 42
D. 48

12. In general, when equipment grounding conductors are installed in a panelboard, a _____ for the equipment grounding conductors shall be secured inside the cabinet.

A. neutral terminal bar
B. ungrounded terminal bar
C. equipment grounding terminal bar
D. bonding jumper

13. When a switchboard or panelboard is supplied from a 4-wire, delta connected system and the grounded conductor is also present, the phase or busbar having the higher voltage to ground, "high-leg," shall be identified as _____ in color.

A. red
B. white
C. green
D. orange

14. For other than a totally enclosed switchboard, a space of NOT less than _____ shall be provided between the top of the switchboard and and combustible material.

A. 24 inches
B. 36 inches
C. 48 inches
D. 18 inches

15. For the purpose of maintaining and servicing a 3-phase, 4-wire, 208 volt panelboard, a working clearance of at LEAST _____ shall be maintained in front of the panelboard.

A. 3 feet
B. 2½ feet
C. 3½ feet
D. 4 feet

ARTICLE 410 - LUMINAIRES, LAMPHOLDERS, and LAMPS
****

16. A _____ shall NOT be located within a zone measured 3 ft. horizontally and 8 ft. vertically from the top of a bathtub rim or shower stall threshold.

    I. recessed luminaire
    II. lighting track

A. I only
B. II only
C. neither I nor II
D. both I and II

17. Branch-circuit conductors within 3 inches of a ballast, installed in a ballast compartment of a luminaire, shall have a temperature rating of NOT less than _____ unless supplying a luminaire listed and marked suitable for a different insulation temperature.

A. 105° C
B. 90° C
C. 75° C
D. 60° C

18. Luminaires shall be installed so that adjacent combustible material is not subjected to temperatures in excess of _____.

A. 60° C
B. 75° C
C. 110° C
D. 90° C

19. Surface mounted incandescent luminaires are permitted to be installed above the door or on the ceiling of a clothes closet, provided there is a MINIMUM clearance of _____ between the luminaire and the nearest shelf.

A. 6 inches
B. 8 inches
C. 12 inches
D. 18 inches

20. Tap conductors for recessed luminaires shall be in a suitable raceway or Type AC or MC cable of at LEAST_____ in length.

A. 1½ feet
B. 2 feet
C. 4 feet
D. 6 feet

21. The NEC® requires recessed portions of luminaire enclosures that are not identified for contact with insulation, to be spaced from combustible material a MINIMUM of:

A. 3/8 in.
B. 1/2 in.
C. 3/4 in.
D. 1 in.

22. The NEC® permits a listed fluorescent luminaire to be cord-and-plug connected if the cord is _____.

A. readily accessible
B. not more than 3 ft. in length
C. visible its entire length
D. GFCI protected

23. All luminaires and lampholders shall be _____.

A. labeled
B. listed
C. approved
D. enclosed

24. In general, luminaires and lampholders shall have no live parts normally exposed to contact. An exception to this rule is where cleat-type lampholders are located at LEAST _____ or more above the floor, they shall be permitted to have exposed terminals.

A. 12 feet
B. 10 feet
C. 7 feet
D. 8 feet

25. A distance of at LEAST _____ horizontally must be maintained between cord-connected luminaires or ceiling-suspended (paddle) fans and bathtub rims or shower stalls.

A. 8 feet
B. 6 feet
C. 4 feet
D. 3 feet

26. A luminaire that weighs at LEAST _____ or more, shall not be supported by the screw shell of a lampholder.

A. 5 lbs.
B. 10 lbs.
C. 6 lbs.
D. 8 lbs.

27. Conductors LONGER than _____ supplying pendant type lampholders shall be twisted together where not cabled together in a listed assembly.

A. 3 feet
B. 4 feet
C. 8 feet
D. 6 feet

28. Where a surface-mounted luminaire containing a ballast, transformer, LED driver, or power-supply, is installed on combustible low-density cellulose fiberboard, it shall be marked for this condition or shall be spaced NOT less than _____ from the surface of the fiberboard.

A. 3/4 in.
B. 1 in.
C. 1¼ in.
D. 1½ in.

29. Where a 24 ft. tall, nonmetallic pole is used to support area landscape lighting luminaires and used as a raceway to enclose supply conductors, the pole shall have a handhole of NOT less than _____ with a cover suitable for use in wet locations to provide access to supply terminations within the pole or pole base.

A. 2 in. x 4 in.
B. 4 in. x 4 in.
C. 2 in. x 6 in.
D. 4 in. x 6 in.

30. Thermal insulation shall not be installed above a recessed luminaire or within at LEAST _____ of the recessed luminaires enclosure, transformer, LED driver, or power-supply, unless the luminaire is identified as Type IC for insulation contact.

A. 2 inches
B. 3 inches
C. 4 inches
D. 3½ inches

ARTICLE 422 - APPLIANCES
****

31. What is the MAXIMUM overcurrent protection rating allowed for infrared heating lamps used on commercial or industrial applications?

A. 30 amperes
B. 40 amperes
C. 50 amperes
D. 20 amperes

32. Conductors supplying fixed storage-type water heaters having a capacity of not over 120 gallons shall have a branch-circuit rating of NOT less than _____ of the nameplate rating of the water heater.

A. 80 percent
B. 100 percent
C. 150 percent
D. 125 percent

33. The MAXIMUM allowable length of flexible cord identified for use of connecting residential kitchen waste disposers is _____.

A. 18 inches
B. 24 inches
C. 36 inches
D. 48 inches

34. What is the MAXIMUM allowable cord length for a cord-and-plug connected dishwasher installed under a kitchen counter in a residence?

A. 1½ feet
B. 2 feet
C. 3 feet
D. 4 feet

35. If a branch-circuit is supplying a single nonmotor-operated appliance, such as an electric range or a water heater, and the appliance is rated over 13.3 amperes, the overcurrent device rating protecting the appliance shall NOT exceed _____ of the nameplate rating of the appliance. Where this percentage of the appliance rating does not correspond to a standard overcurrent device ampere rating, the next higher standard rating shall be permitted.

A. 100 percent
B. 125 percent
C. 115 percent
D. 150 percent

36. Cord-and-plug connected vending machines located indoors in the open area of a retail shopping mall are required to have _____.

A. AFCI protection only
B. GFCI protection only
C. both GFCI & AFCI protection
D. none of these

37. For permanently connected appliances rated at NOT over 300 volt-amperes or _____, the branch-circuit switch shall be permitted to serve as the disconnecting means.

A. 1/8 hp
B. 1/4 hp
C. 1/2 hp
D. 3/4 hp

38. When sizing the overcurrent protection for a single non-motor operated appliance, which of the following should NOT be taken into consideration?

A. The length of time the appliance operates.
B. The full-load current marked on the appliances.
C. The voltage rating on the appliances.
D. Where the overcurrent protection selected is not a standard size.

39. Where a central vacuum assembly is located in a storage closet adjacent to the laundry room of a dwelling, accessible non-current-carrying metal parts of the assembly shall be _____.

A. isolated
B. insulated
C. GFCI protected
D. connected to an equipment grounding conductor

ARTICLE 424 - FIXED ELECTRIC SPACE-HEATING EQUIPMENT
****

40. A branch-circuit supplying more than one electric baseboard heater in a residential occupancy shall be rated a MAXIMUM of _____.

A. 15 amperes
B. 20 amperes
C. 30 amperes
D. 50 amperes

41. The ampacity of the branch-circuit conductors to a residential central heating electric furnace shall NOT be less than _____ of the furnace load.

A. 80 percent
B. 100 percent
C. 115 percent
D. 125 percent

42. What is the MAXIMUM overcurrent protection allowed for the protection of resistance type electric space heating equipment?

A. 30 amperes
B. 40 amperes
C. 50 amperes
D. 60 amperes

43. Thermostatically controlled switching devices serving as both controllers and disconnecting means for fixed electric space heating equipment shall _____.

A. be prohibited
B. be located not more than 5 feet above floor level
C. be designed so that the circuit cannot be energized automatically after the device has been manually placed in the "off" position
D. directly open all grounded conductors when manually placed in the "off" position

44. Resistance type heating elements in electric space heating equipment rated for more than 48 amperes and employing such elements shall have the heating elements subdivided, and each subdivided load shall NOT exceed _____.

A. 20 amperes
B. 30 amperes
C. 40 amperes
D. 48 amperes

45. If an electric space heating unit lead wire is blue in color, this indicates the circuit VOLTAGE to be used for the heating unit is _____.

A. 120 volts
B. 208 volts
C. 240 volts
D. 277 volts

46. What is the MINIMUM required clearance of wiring installed above electric space heating cables installed above a heated ceiling?

A. 2 inches
B. 3 inches
C. 4 inches
D. 6 inches

47. Electric space heating cables shall NOT extend beyond the room or area in which they _____.

A. originate
B. terminate
C. provide heat
D. have overcurrent protection

48. Where constant wattage heating cables are installed in concrete floors, the cables shall NOT exceed _____ per linear foot of cable.

A. 30 watts
B. 54 watts
C. 16½ watts
D. 50 watts

ARTICLE 426 - FIXED OUTDOOR ELECTRIC DEICING and SNOW-MELTING EQUIPMENT
****

49. The ampacity of the branch-circuit conductors and the rating or setting of overcurrent protective devices supplying outdoor deicing and snow-melting equipment must NOT be less than _____ of the heaters.

A. 100 percent
B. 115 percent
C. 125 percent
D. 150 percent

50. The MAXIMUM watt density for imbedded outdoor deicing equipment is _____ per sq. ft. of heated area.

A. 50 watts
B. 80 watts
C. 100 watts
D. 120 watts

END OF UNIT TEN
****

UNIT ELEVEN

NEC® QUESTIONS FROM ARTICLE 430 THROUGH ARTICLE 480

The following National Electrical Code® questions are typical of questions encountered on all electricians' exams, based on the above referenced Articles of the Code. Select the best answer from the choices given then review your answers with the answer key at the back of this book.

ARTICLE 430 - MOTORS, MOTOR CIRCUITS, and CONTROLLERS
****

1. For continuous-duty motors, the motor nameplate current rating is used to determine the size of the _____ required for the motor.

A. disconnecting means
B. branch-circuit conductors
C. motor overload protection
D. short-circuit protection

2. If the individual overload protection is omitted when a motor is connected to a branch circuit by means of an attachment plug-and-receptacle or a cord connector, the rating of the 125-volt or 250-volt attachment plug-and-receptacle or cord connector shall be a MAXIMUM of _____.

A. 15 amperes
B. 20 amperes
C. 30 amperes
D. 40 amperes

3. Branch-circuits supplying a continuous-duty, ac motor shall have an ampacity of NOT less than what percent of the motor full-load current rating?

A. 115 percent
B. 125 percent
C. 150 percent
D. 200 percent

4. Disregarding exceptions, the MAXIMUM rating for branch-circuit, short-circuit, and ground-fault protection of a single-phase motor when using a non-time delay fuse is _____ of the full-load current of the motor.

A. 115 percent
B. 125 percent
C. 250 percent
D. 300 percent

5. In general, the disconnecting means for motor circuits rated 600 volts, nominal, or less, shall have an ampere rating of at least what percent of the full-load current rating of the motor supplied?

A. 80 percent
B. 100 percent
C. 115 percent
D. 125 percent

6. Which of the following is NOT required to be marked on the nameplate of a motor?

A. manufacturer's name
B. full-load current
C. overcurrent protection
D. rated temperature rise

7. A reduced voltage transformer for a motor control circuit, located in the controller enclosure, shall be:

A. connected to the load side of the disconnecting means.
B. connected to the line side of the disconnecting means.
C. connected to a separate circuit.
D. remotely mounted.

8. Motor starting rheostats for direct current motors operated from a constant voltage supply, shall be equipped with automatic devices that interrupt the supply before the speed of the motor has fallen to LESS than _____ its normal rate.

A. one-fourth
B. one-third
C. one-half
D. two-thirds

9. On ac circuits, an ac general-use snap switch, suitable for use only on ac circuits, may be used for controlling a stationary motor rated 2 hp or less, if 300 volts or less, NOT exceeding _____ of the ampere rating of the switch at its rated voltage.

A. 50 percent
B. 80 percent
C. 150 percent
D. 125 percent

10. Exposed live parts of motors must be guarded, if they operate at MORE than _____.

A. 50 volts
B. 100 volts
C. 125 volts
D. 150 volts

11. An attachment plug-and-receptacle or cord connector may be permitted to serve as a motor controller if the motor is portable and has a MAXIMUM rating of _____.

A. 1/8 hp
B. 1/4 hp
C. 1/2 hp
D. 1/3 hp

12. Motors are considered to be continuous-duty UNLESS:

A. they are fractional horsepower, non-automatically started.
B. they are incapable of operating continuous full-load under any condition of use.
C. they are used as an industrial process machine.
D. they have a service factor of 1.15 and automatically started.

13. When sizing branch-circuit conductors supplying torque motors, the _____ of the motor shall be used to determine the required ampacity of the conductors.

A. full-load running current
B. full-load stopping current
C. locked-rotor current
D. starting amperage

14. The absolute MAXIMUM rating of an inverse time circuit breaker for branch-circuit, short-circuit and ground-fault protection for a 40 hp, 230 volt, 3-phase motor is _____ of the full-load current of the motor.

A. 175 percent
B. 250 percent
C. 300 percent
D. 400 percent

15. What is the full-load running current of a 208 volt, 3-phase, 20 hp, induction-type, continuous-duty motor?

A. 6.8 amperes
B. 54 amperes
C. 59.4 amperes
D. 62.1 amperes

16. Where a three-phase, 240 volt, 7½ hp, Design B, 50 deg. C temperature rise motor has a FLA of 20 amperes marked on the nameplate, the MAXIMUM overload device used to protect this motor shall be selected to trip at NOT more than _____ of the full-load ampere rating of the motor.

A. 130 percent
B. 125 percent
C. 115 percent
D. 140 percent

17. If the immediate shut down of a motor, over 600 volts, by its overload device would create an unsafe condition, you should _____.

A. use a time-delay overload for orderly shut-down
B. increase the fuse size by 135%
C. use overload relays with varied inverse time characteristics
D. tie the overload device into a supervised alarm, instead of causing the motor to stop

18. Given: A 30 horsepower wound-rotor, induction motor, with no code letter, is to be connected to a 460-volt, 3-phase source. Disregarding all exceptions, the non-time delay fuses for short-circuit protection of the motor branch-circuit, must be rated at a MAXIMUM of _____ of the full-load current of the motor.

A. 125 percent
B. 150 percent
C. 175 percent
D. 250 percent

19. Where two (2) motors, one smaller than the other, are supplied from a common feeder and are interlocked so that only one of them can run at one time, the calculation of the ampacity of the feeder is to be based on _____.

A. the total full-load current of the two motors
B. 125% of the full-load current of the larger of the two
C. the sum of the full-load current of the two, plus 25% of the full-load current of the larger motor
D. 125% of the total full-load current of the two motors

20. In general, a motor disconnecting means must disconnect _____.

A. only the motor
B. only the controller
C. only the control circuit
D. both the motor and controller

21. Where the motor controller also serves as a disconnecting means, it shall open all _____ conductors to the motor.

A. grounded
B. neutral
C. grounding
D. ungrounded

22. Branch-circuits supplying more than one motor shall have an ampacity of at LEAST_____ of the full-load current of the highest rated motor in the group, and 100% of the full-load current of the other motor(s) in the group.

A. 25 percent
B. 80 percent
C. 100 percent
D. 125 percent

23. If a circuit breaker serves as the controller for a motor, and the motor is not in sight of the circuit breaker, the NEC® requires which of the following?

A. The motor to be less than 2 hp.
B. The circuit breaker to be able to be locked in the open position.
C. The motor to be Code letter "E".
D. The circuit breaker to be rated 25,000 AIC.

24. Motors with a marked service factor of not less than 1.15, shall have the running overload protection sized at _____ of the full-load ampere rating indicated on the motor's nameplate, where modification of this value is not required.

A. 115 percent
B. 125 percent
C. 130 percent
D. 140 percent

25. Where determining the MINIMUM required ampacity of the conductors supplying 3-phase motors, other than continuous duty, such as short-time or intermittent duty, the selection of the conductor ampacity is to be based on a percentage of _____.

   I. the motor nameplate current rating
   II. Table 430.250 of the NEC®

A. I only
B. II only
C. either I or II
D. neither I nor II

26. Overload relays and other devices for motor overload protection that are not capable of opening short-circuits or ground-faults shall be protected by a motor short-circuit protector or by _____.

A. an instantaneous trip circuit breaker only
B. fuses or circuit breakers
C. Class CC fuses only
D. a ground-fault circuit-interrupter

ARTICLE 440 - AIR-CONDITIONING and REFRIGERATING EQUIPMENT

27. For overload protection of a hermetic refrigerator motor-compressor, the overload relay shall be selected to trip at NOT more than _____ of the motor-compressor rated load current.

A. 100 percent
B. 115 percent
C. 130 percent
D. 140 percent

28. A cord-and-attachment plug-connected room air conditioner shall NOT exceed _____ of the rating of the branch-circuit where no other loads are supplied.

A. 40 percent
B. 60 percent
C. 80 percent
D. 100 percent

29. Fuses and circuit breakers responsive to motor current are permitted to serve as the branch-circuit and ground-fault protective devices for motor-compressors of air-conditioning equipment. This device shall be rated at NOT more than _____ of the motor-compressor rated-load current.

A. 125 percent
B. 115 percent
C. 150 percent
D. 250 percent

30. Disregarding exceptions, the disconnecting means for refrigeration and air-conditioning equipment must be _____.

   I. within sight of the equipment
   II. readily accessible

A. I only
B. II only
C. either I or II
D. both I and II

31. Where flexible cord is used to supply a 120 volt room air conditioner, the length of the cord shall NOT exceed_____.

A. 4 feet
B. 6 feet
C. 10 feet
D. 12 feet

32. Where flexible cord is used to supply a 120 volt room air conditioner, the rating of the attachment plug-and-receptacle or cord connector shall NOT exceed _____.

A. 15 amperes
B. 20 amperes
C. 30 amperes
D. 40 amperes

33. The rating of the branch-circuit, short-circuit and ground-fault protective device for individual hermetic motor-compressors, shall not be required to be LESS than _____.

A. 10 amperes
B. 20 amperes
C. 30 amperes
D. 15 amperes

ARTICLE 445 - GENERATORS
****

34. Each ac generator shall be provided with a nameplate giving the manufacturer's name and _____.

A. the kW rating
B. the rated frequency
C. the number of phases
D. all of these

35. Disregarding exceptions, the ampacity of phase conductors from the generator terminals to the first overcurrent device shall NOT be less than _____ of the nameplate current rating of the generator.

A. 100 percent
B. 115 percent
C. 125 percent
D. 150 percent

36. Live parts of generators operated at MORE than _____ to ground shall not be exposed to accidental contact where accessible to unqualified persons.

A. 50 volts
B. 120 volts
C. 150 volts
D. all of these voltages

ARTICLE 450 - TRANSFORMERS and TRANSFORMER VAULTS
****

37. In compliance with the NEC®, what is the MINIMUM sill or curb height of a transformer vault doorway?

A. 4 inches
B. 3 inches
C. 6 inches
D. 8 inches

38. A dry-type transformer of LESS than 600 volts and _____ is permitted to be installed in a hollow space of a building, such as an accessible ceiling, provided there is adequate ventilation.

A. 25 kVA
B. 37½ kVA
C. 50 kVA
D. 112½ kVA

39. Transformers rated at LEAST _____ or larger shall be provided with a nameplate giving the name of the manufacturer, rated kVA, frequency, primary and secondary voltage and impedance.

A. 112½ kVA
B. 25 kVA
C. 50 kVA
D. 60 kVA

40. In general and where installed indoors, individual dry-type transformers of more than 112½ kVA shall be installed in a transformer room of fire-resistant construction having a MINIMUM fire resistance rating of _____.

A. 1 hour
B. 2 hours
C. 3 hours
D. 4 hours

41. Each autotransformer, 600 volts, nominal, or less, shall be protected by an individual overcurrent device installed in series with each ungrounded input conductor. Such overcurrent device shall not be rated or set at not more than what percent of the rated full load input current of the autotransformer?

A. 80 percent
B. 100 percent
C. 115 percent
D. 125 percent

42. Where the rated primary current draw is less than 9 amperes on a 120/240 volt, single-phase transformer, overcurrent protection of NOT more than _____ of the primary current is permitted.

A. 167 percent
B. 150 percent
C. 125 percent
D. 80 percent

ARTICLE 455 - PHASE CONVERTERS
****

43. Given: A 240 volt wye-connected motor derives power from a converted single-phase source. It is desired to connect a 240/120 volt transformer for control of the motor on the load side of the converter. The control transformer must:

A. be connected to the manufactured phase.
B. be disconnected after start-up of the motor.
C. have a separate overcurrent protection device.
D. not be connected to the manufactured phase.

44. When wiring a phase convertor, supplying variable loads, the ampacity of the single-phase conductors on the supply side shall NOT be less than _____ of the phase convertor's single-phase input full-load amperes.

A. 100 percent
B. 115 percent
C. 125 percent
D. 140 percent

45. Means shall be provided to disconnect simultaneously all _____ single-phase supply conductors to the phase convertor.

I. grounded
II. ungrounded

A. I only
B. II only
C. both I and II
D. either I or II

ARTICLE 460 - CAPACITORS

46. Capacitors containing more than a MINIMUM of _____ of flammable liquid shall be enclosed in vaults or outdoor fenced enclosures.

A. 1 gallon
B. 3 gallons
C. 5 gallons
D. 6 gallons

47. For circuits of 600 volts or less, the ampacity of capacitor circuit conductors shall NOT be less than _____ of the rated current of the capacitor.

A. 115 percent
B. 125 percent
C. 135 percent
D. 80 percent

48. For circuits of 600 volts or less, where a motor installation includes a capacitor connected on the load side of the motor overload device, the rating or setting of the motor over-load device shall be based on _____.

A. the improved power factor of the motor circuit
B. 125% of the ampacity of the circuit conductors
C. 135% of the motor nameplate rating
D. 135% of the capacitor nameplate current rating

ARTICLE 480 - STORAGE BATTERIES
****

49. In locations where batteries are stored, provisions shall be made for the ventilation of the gases from the batteries to prevent _____.

A. corrosion
B. electrolysis
C. electro-magnetic induction
D. the accumulation of an explosive mixture

50. Each vented cell of a storage battery shall be equipped with _____ that is/are designed to prevent destruction of the cell due to ignition of gases within the cell by an external spark or flame under normal operating conditions.

A. pressure relief
B. fluid level indicators
C. a flame arrester
D. a fluid level valve

END OF UNIT ELEVEN
****

UNIT TWELVE

NEC® QUESTIONS FROM ARTICLE 500 THROUGH ARTICLE 516

The following National Electrical Code® questions are typical of questions encountered on all electricians' exams, based on the above referenced Articles of the Code. Select the best answer from the choices given then review your answers with the answer key at the back of this book.

ARTICLE 500 - HAZARDOUS LOCATIONS, CLASSES I, II, and III, DIVISIONS 1 and 2
****

1. Industrial atmospheres containing combustible metal dust such as aluminum or magnesium are considered to be in a Class II, _____ hazardous location.

A. Group C
B. Group D
C. Group E
D. Group F

2. The interior of an exhaust duct that is used to vent vapors from a paint booth is classified as a _____ location.

A. Class I, Division 1
B. Class I, Division 2
C. Class II, Division 1
D. Class II, Division 2

3. Classified locations where combustible dust is in the air under normal operating conditions and in quantities sufficient to produce explosive or ignitible mixtures, are designated as _____ hazardous locations.

A. Class I, Division 1
B. Class I, Division 2
C. Class II, Division 1
D. Class II, Division 2

4. Hazardous locations where ignitible concentrations of flammable liquid-produced vapors or combustible liquid-produced vapors exist under normal operating conditions are considered to be designated as _____ classified locations.

A. Class II, Division 2
B. Class II, Division 1
C. Class I, Division 2
D. Class I, Division 1

5. Where a panelboard enclosure is to be installed in an area where easily ignitible fibers are present in the air, but NOT in such quantities sufficient to produce ignitible mixtures, the panelboard enclosure shall be classified, as MINIMUM, approved for use in a _____ location.

A. Class I
B. Class II
C. Class III
D. non-classified

6. The interior of a paint booth is classified as a _____ hazardous location.

A. Class II, Division 1
B. Class I, Division 1
C. Class I, Division 2
D. Class II, Division 2

7. Explosionproof apparatus is required for equipment located in _____ locations.

A. Class I, Division 1 or Division 2
B. Class I, Division 3
C. Class II, Division 1 or Division 2
D. Class III, Division 1 or Division 2

8. Where installed in Class II, Division 2 locations, all panelboard enclosures housing overcurrent devices shall be _____.

A. explosionproof
B. watertight
C. gastight
D. dusttight

9. For field wiring connections, NPT threaded entries into explosionproof equipment shall be made up with at LEAST _____ threads fully engaged.

A. four
B. five
C. three
D. six

10. Where explosionproof equipment is provided with metric threaded entries, which of the following methods is approved to adapt the entries from the metric to NPT threads?

A. Approved adapters from the metric threads to NPT threads shall be used.
B. Tap the metric threaded entries to NPT threads.
C. Thread the conduit with metric threads.
D. All of these are approved methods.

ARTICLE 501 - CLASS I LOCATIONS
****

11. Enclosures in a Class I, Division 1 location containing components that have arcing devices, must have an approved seal located within at LEAST _____ of each conduit entering or leaving such enclosures.

A. 12 inches
B. 18 inches
C. 24 inches
D. 30 inches

12. Where the NEC® requires a conduit seal in each conduit run leaving a Class I, Division 1 location, the conduit seal is permitted on either side of the boundary, and WITHIN _____ of such location's boundary.

A. 20 feet
B. 25 feet
C. 10 feet
D. 15 feet

13. Where installing trade size 1/2 in. threaded rigid metal conduit (RMC) in a Class I location and a conduit seal is required, the MINIMUM thickness of the sealing compound shall NOT be less than _____.

A. 3/8 in.
B. 1/2 in.
C. 5/8 in.
D. 3/4 in.

14. Flexible metal conduit (FMC) with listed fittings is approved for use in which, if any, of the following listed hazardous locations?

I. Class I, Division 1
II. Class I, Division 2

A. I only
B. II only
C. both I and II
D. neither I nor II

15. Disregarding exceptions, bonding between Class I locations and the point of grounding for service equipment may be done by _____.

A. double locknuts
B. bonding jumpers
C. insulated bushings
D. metal raceways

16. For a hazardous location sealing fitting, what is the MAXIMUM percentage of conductor fill as allowed by the NEC®?

A. 25 percent
B. 40 percent
C. 51 percent
D. 60 percent

17. Liquidtight flexible metal conduit (LFMC) is approved for use as a sole equipment grounding conductor and the bonding jumper is permitted to be deleted when installed in Class I locations, if the liquidtight metal conduit is _____ or less in length, and the overcurrent protection in the circuit is limited to _____ or less.

A. 10 ft. – 20 amperes
B. 10 ft. – 15 amperes
C. 6 ft. – 20 amperes
D. 6 ft. – 10 amperes

18. Where located in Class I, Division 1 locations, transformers containing oil or a liquid that will burn shall be _____.

A. enclosed in a fence
B. installed in vaults only
C. identified for Class I locations
D. installed in a fire-resistant room

ARTICLE 502 - CLASS II LOCATIONS
****

19. In Class II, Division 1 and 2 locations, the NEC® permits the use of _____, as an approved method of bonding.

A. bonding jumpers with approved fittings
B. double lock-nuts only
C. double lock-nuts with bushings
D. any of the above methods

20. Disregarding exceptions, which one of the following listed wiring methods is permitted for use in a grain elevator?

A. Type MC cable
B. Type NMB cable
C. Type MI cable
D. Type AC cable

21. Where a horizontal raceway enters a dust-ignition proof enclosure from one that is not dust-ignition proof, the raceway is not required to have a seal-off fitting if it is at LEAST _____ in length.

A. 18 inches
B. 60 inches
C. 120 inches
D. 24 inches

22. An enclosure for a disconnecting means installed in a Class II, Division 2 location shall be _____ or otherwise identified for the location.

A. dusttight
B. heavy-duty type
C. raintight
D. general-duty type

23. In Class II, Division 1 hazardous locations, an approved method of connection of conduit to boxes is _____.

A. compression fittings
B. threaded bosses
C. welding
D. none of these

24. Where located in Class II, Division 1 locations, transformers containing oil or a liquid that will burn shall be _____.

A. enclosed in a fence
B. double-insulated
C. installed in vaults only
D. installed in a fire-resistant room having a rating of not less than 3 hours

25. In Class II, Division 1 locations, where pendant mounted luminaires are suspended by rigid metal conduit (RMC) and a means for flexibility is not provided, the RMC shall have a length of NOT more than _____.

A. 12 inches
B. 18 inches
C. 24 inches
D. 30 inches

ARTICLE 503 - CLASS III LOCATIONS
****

26. A luminaire installed in a Class III location that may be exposed to physical damage shall be protected by a _____ guard.

A. substantial
B. suitable
C. metal
D. polyvinyl

27. An approved wiring method for Class III, Division 1 locations is _____.

   I. rigid polyvinyl chloride conduit (PVC)
   II. electrical metallic tubing (EMT)

A. I only
B. II only
C. both I and II
D. neither I nor II

28. All circuit breakers, switches and motor controllers installed in Class III locations shall be provided with _____ enclosures.

A. raintight
B. nonmetallic
C. watertight
D. dusttight

ARTICLE 511 - COMMERCIAL GARAGES, REPAIR and STORAGE
****

29. A stockroom in a commercial garage is considered to be _____ where effectively cut off by unpierced walls or solid partitions from the garage area.

A. unclassified
B. Class I, Division 1
C. hazardous
D. Class I, Division 2

30. Where ventilation is not provided for a pit in the floor of a major auto repair garage, any pit or depression below floor level is classified as a _____ location that extends up to the floor level.

A. Class I, Division 1
B. Class I, Division 2
C. Class II, Division 1
D. Class II, Division 2

31. In lubrication or service rooms of a major commercial auto repair garage, the area up to a level of 18 inches above the floor shall be considered unclassified where there is mechanical ventilation providing a MINIMUM of _____ changes per hour or one cubic foot per minute of exchanged air for each square foot of the floor area.

A. two
B. four
C. five
D. six

32. In a commercial garage work area, which of the following receptacles, if any, are required to have GFCI protection?

    I. 15 ampere general purpose receptacles for hand tools and portable lighting.
    II. 20 ampere receptacles serving electrical diagnostic equipment only.

A. I only
B. II only
C. both I and II
D. neither I nor II

33. Which of the following wiring methods is/are approved for use for fixed wiring in an area above Class I locations in a commercial garage?

A. Type MI cable
B. Type TC cable
C. Type MC cable
D. All of these are approved.

34. Where open type fluorescent luminaires are permanently mounted over lanes in which vehicles are commonly driven in a commercial garage, the luminaires shall be located NOT less than _____ above the garage floor level.

A. 8 feet
B. 10 feet
C. 14 feet
D. 12 feet

35. Receptacle outlets located 12 inches above the floor in a major vehicle repair garage, where ventilation is not provided, are classified as being in a _____ hazardous (classified) location.

A. Class I, Division 1
B. Class I, Division 2
C. Class II, Division 1
D. Class II, Division 2

36. Where portable lighting equipment is located in Class I locations of commercial garages, the lampholders shall NOT be _____.

A. equipped with a hook
B. of conductive material
C. supplied with a cord
D. switched

ARTICLE 514 - MOTOR FUEL DISPENSING FACILITIES
****

37. When wiring gasoline fuel dispensing pumps, the first fitting that should be installed in the raceway that emerges from below ground or concrete, into the base of the gasoline dispenser is a/an _____.

A. automatic cut-off valve
B. sealing fitting
C. disconnect
D. no fittings of any kind are permitted in this location

38. Conductors leading to a gasoline fuel dispensing unit shall be _____.

A. provided with a switch
B. red in color
C. orange in color
D. insulated with type THWN insulation

39. Where rigid PVC conduit is installed underground to serve a gasoline dispensing unit, threaded rigid metal conduit or threaded steel intermediate metal conduit shall be used for the LAST _____ of the underground run to where the conduit emerges.

A. 2 feet
B. 4 feet
C. 5 feet
D. 6 feet

40. The emergency controls for attended self-service gasoline stations or convenience stores must be located NOT more than _____ from the fuel dispensers.

A. 20 feet
B. 25 feet
C. 75 feet
D. 100 feet

41. The NEC® considers the area around the fuel dispensing pumps in a service station to be a hazardous location. This area extends to a height of 18 inches above grade, and up to a distance from the enclosure of the dispensing pump of _____.

A. 5 feet
B. 10 feet
C. 16 feet
D. 20 feet

42. A multi-wire branch circuit supplying a gasoline fuel dispensing pump shall be provided with a switch that will disconnect _____.

A. only one ungrounded conductor
B. all of the ungrounded supply conductors only
C. only the neutral (grounded) conductor
D. the grounded conductor and all of the ungrounded supply conductors

43. Where a service station has a restroom that does NOT open to the working area, the restroom is classified as a _____ location.

A. non-classified
B. Class I, Division 2
C. Class II, Division 2
D. Class II, Division 1

44. The upward discharging vent of an underground fuel tank of motor fuel dispensing facilities is classified as a Class I, Division 1 location WITHIN _____ of the open end of the vent.

A. 8 feet
B. 6 feet
C. 5 feet
D. 3 feet

ARTICLE 515 - BULK STORAGE PLANTS
****

45. Where rigid PVC conduit is buried underground about a bulk storage plant, the conduit is required to have NOT less than _____ of cover.

A. 1½ feet
B. 2 feet
C. 3 feet
D. 4 feet

46. In a bulk storage plant, the space between 3 feet and _____ of the open end of an aboveground tank vent and extending in all directions is classified as a Class I, Division 1 hazardous location.

A. 6 feet
B. 5 feet
C. 8 feet
D. 10 feet

47. Where fixed wiring above bulk storage tanks is installed in PVC conduit, the PVC conduit shall be _____.

A. Schedule 20
B. Schedule 40
C. Schedule 80
D. Schedule 100

ARTICLE 516 - SPRAY APPLICATION, DIPPING, and COATING PROCESSES
****

48. Illumination of spray booths through glass panels is permitted provided _____.

   I. the panel is of a material or protected so that breakage is unlikely
   II. the panel effectively isolates the Class I location from the area in which the lighting unit is located

A. I only
B. II only
C. either I or II
D. both I and II

49. In the spray area of a paint booth, which of the following, if any, is/are required to be grounded?

   I. Noncurrent-carrying metal parts of the spray booth.
   II. Paint containers and hose connectors.

A. I only
B. II only
C. both I and II
D. neither I nor II

50. The area around an open-face paint spray booth is considered to be a Class I, Division 2 hazardous location and shall extend NOT less than _____ horizontally from the paint spray booth, when the exhaust ventilation system is NOT interlocked with the spray application equipment.

A. 5 feet
B. 10 feet
C. 20 feet
D. 25 feet

END OF UNIT TWELVE
****

UNIT THIRTEEN

NEC® QUESTIONS FROM ARTICLE 517 THROUGH ARTICLE 550

The following National Electrical Code® questions are typical of questions encountered on all electricians' exams, based on the above referenced Articles of the Code. Select the best answer from the choices given then review your answers with the answer key at the back of this book.

ARTICLE 517 - HEALTH CARE FACILITIES
****

1. Each patient bed location within a critical care area of a hospital shall be provided with a MINIMUM of _____ receptacles.

A. two
B. four
C. six
D. eight

2. In general, each patient bed location within a general care area of a health care facility shall be provided with at LEAST _____ receptacles.

A. two
B. four
C. six
D. eight

3. Luminaires installed MORE than _____ above the floor in patient care areas of health care facilities shall not be required to be grounded by an insulated equipment grounding conductor.

A. 6 feet
B. 6½ feet
C. 7 feet
D. 7½ feet

4. In general, which of the following MUST be provided at a patient bed location used for general care in a hospital?

A. Circuit on normal system.
B. Circuit on emergency system.
C. "Hospital-grade" receptacles
D. All of these must be provided.

5. In a health care facility, low voltage electrical equipment that is likely to become energized that is frequently in contact with the bodies of patients must be moisture resistance, be approved as intrinsically safe, double-insulated, or operate on a voltage of _____ or less.

A. 10 volts
B. 24 volts
C. 100 volts
D. 120 volts

6. The critical branch of the hospital emergency system shall provide power to all the operating rooms and all _____.

    I. emergency room treatment areas
    II. nurses stations

A. I only
B. II only
C. both I and II
D. neither I nor II

7. The normal and essential branch-circuit panelboards serving patient care areas of a health care facility must have the equipment grounding terminal buses connected together with an insulated continuous conductor NOT smaller than _____.

A. 12 AWG
B. 6 AWG
C. 10 AWG
D. 8 AWG

8. A hospital isolated power system is a system powered by _____.

A. an isolating transformer or line isolation monitor
B. a transformer or batteries
C. a generator or transformer
D. a monitor or transistor

9. For hospitals, the life safety branch of the emergency system shall be installed and connected to the alternate power source so that all functions for the emergency system shall be automatically restored to operation WITHIN _____ after the interruption of the normal source.

A. 30 seconds
B. 10 seconds
C. 20 seconds
D. 60 seconds

10. The critical branch of the emergency system in a health care facility is NOT required to provide lighting for _____.

A. medication preparation areas
B. pharmacy dispensing areas
C. telephone equipment rooms
D. electrical equipment rooms

11. According to the NEC®, what are the two branches of the hospital emergency system?

A. The emergency branch and the standby branch.
B. The life safety branch and the critical branch.
C. The normal branch and the alternate branch.
D. The essential branch and the non-essential branch.

12. Locations in health care facilities where flammable anesthetics are used, the entire area above the floor up to a level of _____ shall be considered to be a Class I, Division 1 location.

A. 10 feet
B. 6 feet
C. 8 feet
D. 5 feet

13. The ampacity requirements for a disconnecting means of X-ray equipment shall be based on _____ of the input required for the momentary rating of the equipment, if greater than the long-term rating.

A. 125 percent
B. 115 percent
C. 80 percent
D. 50 percent

14. In a hospital, what equipment is required to supply the alternate power serving the critical and life safety branch from the essential electrical system?

A. isolating transformer
B. generator
C. inverter
D. converter

15. In health care facilities, X-ray equipment supplied by a branch-circuit rated at NOT more than _____ may be served by a hard-service cord with a suitable attachment plug.

A. 15 amperes
B. 20 amperes
C. 30 amperes
D. 60 amperes

16. Isolating transformers in health care facilities shall operate at a voltage NOT to exceed _____ between conductors.

A. 120 volts
B. 250 volts
C. 480 volts
D. 600 volts

ARTICLE 518 – ASSEMBLY OCCUPANCIES
****

17. According to the NEC®, which of the following listed is NOT considered to be an *assembly occupancy*?

A. Dining facilities
B. Museums
C. Restaurants
D. Supermarkets

18. A hospital conference room is considered to be an *assembly occupancy* if it is designed for the assembly of at LEAST _____ people.

A. 25
B. 50
C. 75
D. 100

19. Temporary cord approved for hard-usage is permitted to be laid on floors in exhibition halls used for display booths in trade shows, provided it is _____.

A. not over 150 volts between conductors
B. not a branch-circuit
C. protected from contact by the general public
D. type RD cable

20. Which one of the wiring methods is NOT approved for use in assembly locations unless encased in concrete?

A. Electrical metallic tubing (EMT)
B. Schedule 80 PVC conduit
C. Type MC cable
D. Type AC cable

ARTICLE 520 - THEATERS, AUDIENCE AREAS of MOTION PICTURE and TELEVISION STUDIOS, and SIMILAR LOCATIONS
****

21. When installing footlights or border lighting in theaters, the luminaires shall be arranged so that no branch-circuit will carry a load to EXCEED _____.

A. 10 amperes
B. 20 amperes
C. 15 amperes
D. 30 amperes

22. The branch-circuit supplying an autotransformer-type dimmer installed in theaters and similar places shall NOT exceed _____ between conductors.

A. 480 volts
B. 277 volts
C. 240 volts
D. 150 volts

23. Receptacles for electrical equipment or fixtures on stages shall be rated in _____.

A. VA
B. watts
C. amperes
D. hp

24. In a TV studio where dimmers are installed in ungrounded conductors, each dimmer shall have overcurrent protection NOT greater than _____ of the dimmer rating and shall be disconnected from all ungrounded conductors when the switch or circuit breaker supplying such dimmer is in the open position.

A. 125 percent
B. 150 percent
C. 175 percent
D. 200 percent

25. Footlights, border lights, or portable strip lights shall be wired with conductors that have an insulation rating of NOT less than _____.

A. 90° C
B. 125° C
C. 75° C
D. 140° C

26. Which of the following listed raceways is NOT permitted to be installed in theaters and similar locations unless it is encased in concrete?

A. electrical metallic tubing (EMT)
B. flexible metal conduit (FMC)
C. rigid Schedule 40 PVC conduit
D. rigid metal conduit (RMC)

ARTICLE 525 - CARNIVALS, CIRCUSES, FAIRS and SIMILAR EVENTS
****

27. Carnival rides, amusement attractions, and similar portable structures shall be maintained NOT less than _____ in any direction from overhead conductors operating at 600 volts or less, except for the conductors supplying the ride, attraction, or portable structure.

A. 15 feet
B. 20 feet
C. 25 feet
D. 30 feet

28. Each portable structure or ride of a carnival, circus, fair, or similar event shall be provided with a fused disconnect switch or circuit breaker located within sight and within at LEAST _____ of the operator's station.

A. 6 feet
B. 10 feet
C. 20 feet
D. 50 feet

29. Single conductor cable shall be permitted to be installed at fairs, carnivals, or similar events ONLY in sizes of _____ or larger.

A. 6 AWG
B. 2 AWG
C. 8 AWG
D. 4 AWG

30. Termination boxes installed outdoors at a carnival, fair, or circus shall be of weatherproof construction and mounted so that the bottom of the enclosure is NOT less than _____ above ground.

A. 4 inches
B. 6 inches
C. 8 inches
D. 12 inches

31. At a carnival, where multiple services supply portable rides or attractions located LESS than _____ apart, the equipment grounding conductors of all the services shall be bonded to the same grounding electrode system.

A. 15 feet
B. 12 feet
C. 20 feet
D. 22½ feet

32. At carnivals, fairs, and similar events, service equipment shall not be installed in a location that is accessible to unqualified person, UNLESS the equipment _____.

A. has a voltage to ground of not more than 125 volts
B. is provided with GFCI protection
C. is lockable
D. is installed at a height of more than 6 feet

ARTICLE 530 - MOTION PICTURE and TELEVISION STUDIOS and SIMILAR LOCATIONS
****

33. On a movie set, cables and cords supplied through plugging boxes shall be of _____.

   I. copper
   II. copper-coated aluminum

A. I only
B. II only
C. either I or II
D. neither I nor II

34. The wiring for portable stage set lighting, where not subject to physical damage, shall be done with listed _____ flexible cords and cables.

   I. hard usage
   II. extra-hard usage

A. I only
B. II only
C. either I or II
D. neither I nor II

35. Stage cables for stage set lighting shall be protected by overcurrent devices set at NOT more than _____ of the ampacity of the conductor.

A. 100 percent
B. 125 percent
C. 150 percent
D. 400 percent

ARTICLE 547 - AGRICULTURAL BUILDINGS
****

36. In a farm building where livestock is housed and an equipotential plane system is required because wire mesh or other conductive elements are embedded in or placed under concrete and bonded to metal structures that may become energized. The equipotential plane is necessary to prevent a difference in _____ developing within the plane.

A. wattage
B. current
C. resistance
D. voltage

37. Which of the following wiring methods is NOT approved for use in an agricultural establishment?

A. Type NMC cable
B. Type UF cable
C. Type MC cable
D. Type NMB cable

38. When using Type UF cable as a wiring method in an agricultural building, the cable shall be secured within at LEAST _____ of each outlet box.

A. 6 inches
B. 8 inches
C. 12 inches
D. 10 inches

39. The MINIMUM size bonding conductor required to bond an equipotential plane in an agricultural building is size _____ copper.

A. 10 AWG
B. 8 AWG
C. 6 AWG
D. 4 AWG

40. Luminaires installed in a poultry house that may be exposed to water from condensation or cleansing shall be _____.

A. raintight
B. drip-proof
C. watertight
D. listed for use in wet locations

41. A disconnecting means installed at the distribution point where two or more agricultural buildings are supplied shall NOT be required to _____.

A. be grounded
B. contain overcurrent protection
C. contain a grounded conductor
D. be rated for the calculated load

ARTICLE 550 - MOBILE HOMES, MANUFACTURED HOMES and MOBILE HOME PARKS

42. Mobile home service equipment shall be rated at NOT less than _____ at 120/240 volts, single-phase for each mobile home to be supplied.

A. 60 amperes
B. 100 amperes
C. 150 amperes
D. 200 amperes

43. Where calculating the total demand load for a small mobile home park that has four (4) mobile home lots, according to the NEC®, the demand factor to be applied to the park ungrounded (phase) service-entrance conductors is _____.

A. 100 percent
B. 80 percent
C. 50 percent
D. 39 percent

44. A main service disconnect for an individual mobile home is permitted to be:

A. installed at any accessible location within the mobile home.
B. mounted on the exterior wall of the mobile home.
C. mounted on a pole, not more than 30 ft. from the exterior wall of the mobile home.
D. mounted on a pole, not more than 40 ft. from the exterior wall of the mobile home.

45. When installing 120/240 volt, single-phase, service-entrance conductors in a conduit mast for a 100 ampere service to supply a mobile home, the raceway shall contain a MINIMUM of _____ insulated conductors.

A. two
B. three
C. four
D. five

46. For enclosing a mobile home supply cord, what is the MAXIMUM trade size conduit permitted between the branch circuit panelboard of a mobile home and the underside of a mobile home floor?

A. 1 in.
B. 1¼ in.
C. 1½ in.
D. 2 in.

47. Mobile home park electrical wiring systems must be calculated on the basis of a MINIMUM of _____ (at 120/240 volts) for each mobile home lot, or the calculated load of the largest typical mobile home the lot will accommodate.

A. 15,000 VA
B. 16,000 VA
C. 20,000 VA
D. 10,000 VA

48. The overall length of a power supply cord of a mobile home shall NOT exceed _____.

A. 21 feet
B. 40½ feet
C. 36½ feet
D. 50 feet

49. In general, the power supply cord to a mobile home shall have a MAXIMUM rating of _____.

A. 50 amperes
B. 60 amperes
C. 100 amperes
D. 200 amperes

50. An outdoor mobile home disconnecting means shall be installed so the bottom of the enclosure containing the disconnecting means is NOT less than _____ above finished grade or working platform.

A. 2 feet
B. 3 feet
C. 4 feet
D. 5 feet

END OF UNIT THIRTEEN
****

UNIT FOURTEEN

NEC® QUESTIONS FROM ARTICLE 551 THROUGH ARTICLE 630

The following National Electrical Code® questions are typical of questions encountered on all electricians' exams, based on the above referenced Articles of the Code. Select the best answer from the choices given then review your answers with the answer key at the back of this book.

ARTICLE 551 - RECREATIONAL VEHICLES and RECREATIONAL VEHICLE PARKS
****

1. What percent of electrical supplied spaces in a recreational vehicle park must be equipped with a 50-ampere, 125/250 volt receptacle outlet?

A. 70 percent
B. 20 percent
C. 30 percent
D. 100 percent

2. Disregarding exceptions, the working clearance for a distribution panelboard installed in a RV shall be NO less than _____ with the RV in the setup mode.

   I. 24 in wide
   II. 30 in. deep

A. I only
B. II only
C. both I and II
D. either I or II

3. Electrical services and feeders of a RV park shall be calculated on the basis of NOT less than _____ per site equipped with 50-ampere, 208Y/120, or 120/240 volt supply facilities.

A. 3,600 VA
B. 2,400 VA
C. 6,900 VA
D. 9,600 VA

4. When calculating the demand load on a recreational vehicle park, the correct demand factor to be applied to the RV park service-entrance conductors for a RV park having 40 sites is _____.

A. 41 percent
B. 36 percent
C. 40 percent
D. 35 percent

5. The electrical supply equipment at a RV site shall be located NOT less than _____ above the ground.

A. 2 feet
B. 3 feet
C. 4 feet
D. 6½ feet

6. Every recreational vehicle site with electrical power shall be equipped with at LEAST one _____ receptacle.

A. 15 ampere, 125 volt
B. 30 ampere, 125 volt
C. 50 ampere, 125/250 volt
D. 20 ampere, 125 volt

7. In a recreational vehicle park, all switches, circuit breakers, and receptacles located in wet locations shall be _____.

A. raintight
B. weatherproof
C. weather-resistant
D. watertight

8. In a RV park where direct-buried conductors and cables emerge from a trench and are subject to physical damage, they are required to be protected by approved raceways. Which of the following listed raceways is NOT approved for such protection?

A. Intermediate metal conduit (IMC)
B. Schedule 80 PVC conduit
C. Schedule 40 PVC conduit
D. Rigid Metal Conduit (RMC)

ARTICLE 552 - PARK TRAILERS
****

9. For a trailer to be considered a "park trailer" it must have a gross trailer area NOT exceeding _____ in the set-up mode.

A. 600 square feet
B. 400 square feet
C. 800 square feet
D. 1000 square feet

10. In general, the overall length of a power supply cord of a park trailer shall NOT exceed _____.

A. 12 feet
B. 36½ feet
C. 28 feet
D. 40 feet

11. Disregarding exceptions, for park trailers, the point of entrance of a power-supply cord assembly shall be located within at LEAST _____ of the rear of the trailer.

A. 5 feet
B. 10 feet
C. 15 feet
D. 30 feet

ARTICLE 555 - MARINAS and BOATYARDS
****

12. Which one of the following wiring methods is acceptable for equipment grounding in a boat yard?

A. Threaded rigid metal conduit
B. Insulated copper conductor
C. Rigid nonmetallic tubing
D. Electrical metallic tubing

13. Shore power for boats shall be provided by single receptacles rated NOT less than _____.

A. 15 amperes
B. 20 amperes
C. 30 amperes
D. 50 amperes

14. Where shore power accommodations provide two receptacles specifically for an individual boat slip, and these two receptacles have different voltages, _____ need be used for feeder and service calculations.

A. the kW demand of both receptacles
B. 100% of the kW demand of the smaller receptacle, plus 125% of the kW demand of the larger receptacle
C. 125% of the kW demand of both receptacles
D. only the kW demand of the larger receptacle

15. Where the construction of piers, wharfs or docks is open and motor fuel dispensing stations are present, the area 18 inches above the surface of the dock, pier or wharf and extending 20 feet horizontally in all directions from the outside edge of the fuel dispenser and down to the water level shall be _____.

A. Class I, Division I
B. Class I, Division 2
C. Class II, Division 1
D. Class II, Division 2

16. In regard to marinas and boatyards, the disconnecting means for shore power connections provided to isolate each boat from its supply connection(s), shall be readily accessible and located NOT more than _____ from the receptacle it controls.

A. 30 inches
B. 6 feet
C. 4 feet
D. 10 feet

ARTICLE 590 – TEMPORARY INSTALLATIONS
****

17. Temporary electric power provided for Christmas decorative lighting shall be permitted for a period NOT to extend _____.

A. 30 days
B. 60 days
C. 90 days
D. 60 days after the holiday

18. On a construction site where the assured equipment grounding program is applied, how often must the required tests be performed?

A. Monthly
B. Quarterly
C. Weekly
D. Yearly

19. In general, all 250-volt, 30-ampere, single-phase, twist-lock receptacles supplied from the temporary service of a construction jobsite, shall have _____ protection provided for personnel.

   I. GFCI
   II. AFCI

A. I only
B. II only
C. both I and II
D. either I or II

ARTICLE 600 - ELECTRIC SIGNS and OUTLINE LIGHTING
****

20. A type of electric sign the NEC® does NOT require to be listed if installed in conformance with the Code is a _____ sign.

A. lighted portable
B. traffic signal
C. neon lighted
D. HID lighted

21. Branch-circuits that supply neon tubing installations shall NOT be rated in excess of _____.

A. 30 amperes
B. 20 amperes
C. 40 amperes
D. 15 amperes

22. Branch-circuits that supply outline lighting systems containing incandescent luminaires shall be rated NOT to exceed _____.

A. 15 amperes
B. 20 amperes
C. 30 amperes
D. 50 amperes

23. The disconnecting means shall be _____ of the electric sign or outline lighting that it controls.

   I. within sight or capable of being locked in the open position
   II. within 50 feet

A. I only
B. II only
C. neither I nor II
D. either I or II

24. Where a transformer is installed in the attic of a department store and the transformer serves an exterior electric sign, this installation is allowed by the NEC® if there is an access door of at LEAST _____.

A. 24 in. x 24½ in.
B. 36 in. x 22½ in.
C. 36 in. x 24½ in.
D. 48 in. x 28½ in.

25. Switches and similar devices controlling a transformer in an electric sign shall be rated for controlling inductive loads or must have an ampere rating of NOT less than _____ of the ampere rating of the transformer.

A. 100 percent
B. 200 percent
C. 125 percent
D. 150 percent

26. Where an electric sign is installed in the parking lot of a retail shopping mall and is not protected from physical damage, the NEC® requires the sign to be at LEAST _____ above areas accessible to vehicles.

A. 10 feet
B. 16 feet
C. 12 feet
D. 14 feet

27. Where situated in dry locations, what is the MAXIMUM length allowed for cords supplying mobile or portable electric signs?

A. 10 feet
B. 6 feet
C. 15 feet
D. 25 feet

28. Each commercial building accessible to pedestrians shall have an outside sign circuit rated at LEAST _____ that supplies no other load.

A. 20 amperes
B. 15 amperes
C. 25 amperes
D. 30 amperes

29. A mobile or portable electric sign located in wet locations, shall be provided with _____.

   I. an attachment plug
   II. GFCI protection

A. I only
B. II only
C. both I and II
D. neither I nor II

30. In general, where a 24 ft. tall nonmetallic pole used to support an electric sign encloses branch-circuit conductors, the pole is required to have a handhole of NOT less than _____ at the bottom of the pole, with a cover suitable for use in wet locations.

A. 4 in. x 4 in.
B. 2 in. x 6 in.
C. 2 in. x 4 in.
D. 4 in. x 6 in.

31. Splices in field-installed skeleton tubing high-voltage secondary circuit conductors _____.

A. shall be made in listed enclosures rated over 1000 volts
B. are not permitted
C. are permitted when not in an enclosure
D. shall be made with sleeved crimp-on type connections rated 1000 volts

32. Branch-circuits that supply electric signs containing fluorescent luminaire ballasts shall be rated NOT to exceed _____.

A. 30 amperes
B. 25 amperes
C. 20 amperes
D. 15 amperes

ARTICLE 620 - ELEVATORS, DUMBWAITERS, ESCALATORS, MOVING WALKS, WHEELCHAIR LIFTS, and STAIRWAY CHAIR LIFTS
****

33. The MINIMUM size conductor the NEC® permits for cords used as traveling cables supplying lighting circuits in an elevator car is _____ copper.

A. 16 AWG
B. 12 AWG
C. 14 AWG
D. 10 AWG

34. Elevator driving motors used with a generator field control are rated as _____ duty motors.

A. intermittent
B. continuous
C. variable
D. controlled

35. Trade size 3/8 in. flexible metal conduit (FMC) shall be permitted between control panels and machine motors in elevators if the FMC does NOT exceed _____ in length.

A. 6 feet
B. 8 feet
C. 10 feet
D. 12 feet

36. Vertical runs of wireways installed in elevator shafts, shall be securely supported at intervals NOT exceeding _____.

A. 6 feet
B. 10 feet
C. 12 feet
D. 15 feet

37. All 125-volt, 20-ampere rated receptacles installed _____ are required to be provided with GFCI protection.

   I. on elevator car tops
   II. in elevator machine rooms

A. I only
B. II only
C. both I and II
D. neither I nor II

38. Is flexible cord permitted to supply a sump pump located in an elevator pit?

A. No, only flexible metal conduit is permitted for this type of installation.
B. Yes, if the cord is of hard usage oil-resistant type, of a length not to exceed 6 feet.
C. No, only liquid-tight flexible nonmetallic conduit is permitted for this type of installation.
D. Yes, if the applies voltage does not exceed 125 volts.

39. Unless special permission is granted, main feeders for supplying power to elevators and dumbwaiters shall be installed _____.

A. inside a hoistway
B. outside a hoistway
C. in flexible metallic conduit
D. in rigid metal conduit

ARTICLE 625 – ELECTRIC VEHICLE CHARGING SYSTEMS

****

40. The electric vehicle supply equipment shall be provided with a flexible cable with an overall length of NOT more than _____, unless equipped with a cable management system that is listed as suitable for the purpose.

A. 25 feet
B. 37½ feet
C. 50 feet
D. 75 feet

41. Overcurrent protection for feeders and branch-circuits supplying electric vehicle supply equipment shall be sized for continuous duty and have a rating of NOT less than _____ of the maximum load of the electric vehicle supply equipment.

A. 80 percent
B. 100 percent
C. 115 percent
D. 125 percent

42. Where electric vehicle supply equipment is installed indoors, the coupling means of the equipment shall be located at a height of NOT more than _____ above the floor level.

A. 18 inches
B. 24 inches
C. 48 inches
D. 60 inches

ARTICLE 626 – ELECTRIFIED TRUCK PARKING SPACES

****

43. Electrical services and feeders of electrified truck parking spaces shall be calculated on the basis of NOT less than _____ per electrified truck parking space.

A. 10 kVA
B. 11 kVA
C. 15 kVA
D. 17½ kVA

44. The mounting height of post, pedestal, or raised concrete pad types of electrified truck parking space supply equipment shall be located NOT less than _____ above ground.

A. 2 feet
B. 3 feet
C. 3½ feet
D. 4 feet

45. In general, every electrified truck parking space shall be equipped with _____.

   I. a maximum of three (3) receptacles rated 20 amperes, 125 volts each
   II. one (1) single receptacle rated 30 amperes, 208Y/120 volts or 125/250 volts

A. I only
B. II only
C. both I and II
D. either I or II

ARTICLE 630 - ELECTRIC WELDERS
****

46. When a transformer arc welder is rated for continuous use, the supply conductors to the welder shall have an ampacity of NOT less than _____ of the primary current of the welder.

A. 100 percent
B. 125 percent
C. 95 percent
D. 200 percent

47. A transformer arc welder shall have overcurrent protection rated at NOT more than _____ of the rated primary current of the welder.

A. 100 percent
B. 200 percent
C. 150 percent
D. 300 percent

48. Conductors that supply one or more resistance type welders shall be protected by an overcurrent device rated at NOT more than _____ of the conductor ampacity.

A. 100 percent
B. 125 percent
C. 200 percent
D. 300 percent

49. When a cable tray contains welding cables, a permanent sign shall be attached to the cable tray at intervals NOT greater than _____. The sign shall read: CABLE TRAY FOR WELDING CABLES ONLY.

A. 10 feet
B. 20 feet
C. 50 feet
D. 100 feet

50. The insulation of welding cables intended for used in the secondary circuit of electric welders shall be _____.

A. inflammable
B. weatherproof
C. flame retardant
D. nonflammable

END OF UNIT FOURTEEN

UNIT FIFTEEN

NEC® QUESTIONS FROM ARTICLE 645 THROUGH ARTICLE 680

The following National Electrical Code® questions are typical of questions encountered on all electricians' exams, based on the above referenced Articles of the Code. Select the best answer from the choices given then review your answers with the answer key at the back of this book.

ARTICLE 645 - INFORMATION TECHNOLOGY EQUIPMENT
****

1. Conductors installed under raised floors in data processing rooms supplying branch-circuits to receptacles or field-wired equipment, are permitted to be installed in _____.

A. Type AC cable
B. electrical nonmetallic tubing
C. flexible metal conduit
D. all of these

2. The branch-circuit conductors supplying one or more units of information technology equipment shall have an ampacity of NOT less than what percent of the connected load?

A. 80 percent
B. 100 percent
C. 115 percent
D. 125 percent

3. All exposed non-current-carrying metal parts of an information technology system shall be grounded in accordance with Article 250 of the NEC® or shall be _____.

A. double insulated
B. insulated
C. isolated
D. bonded

4. The NEC® mandates an approved means shall be provided to disconnect power to all electronic equipment and HVAC systems in an information technology equipment room. The control for the disconnecting means _____.

A. shall be located in the electrical equipment room
B. is permitted to be installed in a remote location or in the information technology equipment room at approved readily accessible locations
C. shall be located within 25 feet of the exit doors of the information technology equipment room only
D. shall be located adjacent to the principle exit doors of the information technology equipment room only

5. The accessible portion of abandoned supply circuits and interconnecting cables located in an information technology equipment room shall be removed, UNLESS _____.

A. tagged and identified as abandoned
B. identified as Type CMP
C. contained in a raceway
D. not contained in a raceway

6. A designated information technology equipment room is REQUIRED to be _____.

A. sound-proofed
B. provided with at least two exit doors
C. provided with walls at least 6 inches thick
D. separated from other occupancies by fire-resistant-rated walls, floors, and ceilings

7. Openings around electrical penetrations through a wall of a designated computer room are REQUIRED to be _____.

A. watertight
B. airtight
C. firestopped
D. sound-proofed

8. All exposed non-current-carrying metal parts of an information technology system shall _____ or shall be double insulated.

A. be bonded to the equipment grounding conductor
B. not be bonded to the equipment grounding conductor
C. be bonded to the grounding conductor
D. be isolated

ARTICLE 647 – SENSITIVE ELECTRONIC EQUIPMENT
****

9. In the originating branch-circuit panelboard supplying sensitive electronic equipment, the equipment grounding conductors shall be connected to a grounding bus prominently MARKED_____.

A. WARNING –TECHNICAL POWER
B. TECHNICAL EQUIPMENT GROUND
C. for electronic use only
D. GFCI protected

10. When installing wiring for sensitive electronic equipment, the MAXIMUM voltage to ground is required to be _____.

A. 30 volts
B. 60 volts
C. 120 volts
D. 277 volts

ARTICLE 660 - X-RAY EQUIPMENT
****

11. Stationary X-ray equipment is permitted to be supplied through a suitable attachment plug cap and hard-service cable or cord, if the branch circuit supplying the equipment is NOT rated over _____.

A. 15 amperes
B. 20 amperes
C. 30 amperes
D. 60 amperes

12. The momentary rating for X-ray equipment is based on an operating interval that does NOT exceed _____.

A. 5 seconds
B. 25 seconds
C. 30 seconds
D. 15 seconds

13. When sizing branch-circuit conductors supplying X-ray equipment, the momentary rating of _____ is to be used or 100 percent of the long-term rating, whichever is greater.

A. 25 percent
B. 50 percent
C. 75 percent
D. 80 percent

14. A disconnecting means for X-ray equipment shall have adequate capacity for at LEAST _____ of the input required for the momentary rating of the equipment or 100 percent of the input required for the long-term rating, whichever is greater.

A. 50 percent
B. 75 percent
C. 80 percent
D. 100 percent

15. Conductors of size 18 AWG and 16 AWG shall be permitted for the control and operating circuits of X-ray equipment, when protected by an overcurrent device rated at NOT greater than _____.

A. 10 amperes
B. 15 amperes
C. 7 amperes
D. 20 amperes

ARTICLE 665 - INDUCTION and DIELECTRIC HEATING
****

16. Article 665 of the NEC® addresses the construction and installation of induction and dielectric heating equipment for _____ applications.

   I. medical
   II. industrial

A. I only
B. II only
C. both I and II
D. neither I nor II

17. The disconnecting means for induction and dielectric heating equipment shall be readily accessible and _____.

I. located within sight from the controller
II. capable of being locked in the open position

A. I only
B. II only
C. either I or II
D. both I and II

18. The ampacity of conductors supplying one or more pieces of induction or dielectric heating equipment shall not be less than the sum of the nameplate ratings for the largest group of machines capable of simultaneous operation, PLUS _____ of the standby currents of the remaining machines.

A. 100 percent
B. 125 percent
C. 115 percent
D. 150 percent

ARTICLE 668 - ELECTROLYTIC CELLS
****

19. The provisions of Article 668 of the NEC® addresses electrolytic cells used _____.

I. as a source of electric energy
II. for the production of hydrogen

A. I only
B. II only
C. both I and II
D. neither I nor II

20. Cell line conductors for electrolytic cells shall be of _____ material.

I. aluminum
II. steel

A. I only
B. II only
C. either I or II
D. neither I nor II

21. In the vicinity of electrolytic cell lines, the frames and enclosures of portable electrical equipment used within the cell line working zone shall be permitted to be grounded where the cell line voltage EXCEEDS _____.

A. 200 volts dc
B. 100 volts dc
C. 50 volts dc
D. 60 volts dc

ARTICLE 675 - ELECTRICALLY DRIVEN or CONTROLLED IRRIGATION MACHINES
****

22. An electrically driven or controlled machine, not hand-portable, with one or more motors, and used primarily to transport and distribute water for agricultural purposes is an _____, as defined in the NEC®.

A. irrigation machine
B. electrical watering system
C. automatic water distribution system
D. electrical sprinkling system

23. The NEC® mandates tap conductors to individual motors for irrigation machines to be NOT less than size _____ and not more than 25 feet in length.

A. 16 AWG
B. 14 AWG
C. 12 AWG
D. 10 AWG

24. Irrigation cable shall be secured by straps, hangers or similar fittings at intervals NOT exceeding _____.

A. 10 feet
B. 8 feet
C. 6 feet
D. 4 feet

25. Collector rings of irrigation machines shall have a current rating NOT less than _____ of the full-load current of the largest device served plus the FLC of all other devices served.

A. 80 percent
B. 100 percent
C. 125 percent
D. 150 percent

26. For the selection of branch circuit conductors for center pivot irrigations machines, the ampacity of the conductors shall be equal to 125 percent of the motor nameplate full-load current rating of the largest motor in the group PLUS _____ of the sum of the nameplate FLC of all remaining motors on the branch-circuit.

A. 60 percent
B. 75 percent
C. 80 percent
D. 100 percent

ARTICLE 680 - SWIMMING POOLS, FOUNTAINS, and SIMILAR INSTALLATIONS
****

27. Where a 125-volt, general-purpose receptacle is located in the back yard of a dwelling near a permanently installed swimming pool and the receptacle does not provide power to pool associated equipment, the receptacle shall be located NOT less than _____ from the inside wall of the pool.

A. 5 feet
B. 10 feet
C. 6 feet
D. 20 feet

28. All 15- or 20-ampere, single-phase, 125-volt receptacles located within 20 feet of the edge of a decorative fountain shall be _____.

A. GFCI protected
B. a single receptacle
C. prohibited
D. 24 in. above ground level

29. Junction boxes extending to underwater swimming pool luminaires are required to be located NOT less than _____ horizontally, from the inside wall of the pool unless separated from the pool by a solid fence, wall, or other permanent barrier.

A. 3 feet
B. 4 feet
C. 5 feet
D. 10 feet

30. Totally-enclosed luminaires protected by a GFCI and located above a new indoor swimming pool, shall be installed at a MINIMUM height above the water level of _____.

A. 16 feet
B. 12 feet
C. 10 feet
D. 7½ feet

31. All receptacles located within at LEAST _____ of a therapeutic tub shall be protected by a ground-fault circuit interrupter.

A. 20 feet
B. 10 feet
C. 6 feet
D. 5 feet

32. At least one 125-volt, 15- or 20-ampere, general-purpose receptacle shall be located NOT LESS than _____ from and NOT MORE than _____ from the inside wall of a hot tub installed indoors of a residence.

A. 6 feet – 10 feet
B. 6 feet – 15 feet
C. 5 feet – 10 feet
D. 10 feet – 20 feet

33. Other than low-voltage luminaires not requiring grounding, where a wet-niche luminaire of a swimming pool is supplied by a flexible cord, the equipment grounding conductor shall not be smaller than the supply conductors and NOT smaller than size _____.

A. 8 AWG
B. 10 AWG
C. 12 AWG
D. 16 AWG

34. When grounding the reinforcing steel of a swimming pool, what is the SMALLEST size equipotential bonding conductor permitted for this installation?

A. 12 AWG
B. 10 AWG
C. 8 AWG
D. 6 AWG

35. Flexible cords supplying fixed swimming pool equipment shall NOT exceed _____ in length.

A. 3 feet
B. 6 feet
C. 10 feet
D. 12 feet

36. Switching devices shall be installed at LEAST_____ horizontally from the inside walls of a swimming pool unless separated from the pool by a solid fence, wall or other permanent barrier.

A. 6 feet
B. 5 feet
C. 10 feet
D. 20 feet

37. For other than single-family dwellings, spas and hot tubs are required to have a clearly labeled emergency shutoff or control switch provided. This switch shall be installed at a point readily accessible to the users and NOT less than _____ away and within sight of the spa or hot tub.

A. 12 feet
B. 10 feet
C. 15 feet
D. 5 feet

38. The NEC® mandates all 125-volt, 15- and 20-ampere receptacles located WITHIN _____ or less from the inside walls of a storable pool shall be protected by a ground-fault circuit interrupter.

A. 6 feet
B. 10 feet
C. 20 feet
D. 25 feet

39. In general, when installing an equipment grounding conductor in a conduit serving a swimming pool underwater luminaire, it shall be _____.

A. solid
B. bare
C. a minimum size of 8 AWG
D. insulated copper

40. Which one of the following listed conduits does the NEC® permit to enclose conductors supplying wet-niche underwater pool luminaires?

A. electrical metallic tubing
B. electrical nonmetallic tubing
C. galvanized rigid metal
D. brass rigid metal

41. A single family residence is served with insulated 120/240 volt service drop conductors, supported with a grounded messenger wire from the local utility company. This service drop crosses above the swimming pool; the pool has a diving board that is 5 feet above the water level. The NEC® requires the MINIMUM height above water level for the service drop conductors to be _____.

A. 10 feet
B. 14 feet
C. 22½ feet
D. 19 feet

42. When nonmetallic conduit is used to enclose conductors serving a wet-niche luminaire in a swimming pool, a size _____ insulated copper bonding jumper shall be installed in this conduit, unless a listed low-voltage lighting system is used, not requiring grounding.

A. 12 AWG
B. 10 AWG
C. 8 AWG
D. 6 AWG

43. An indoor installed spa or hot tub shall have receptacles NO closer than _____ horizontally from the inside walls of the unit.

A. 6 feet
B. 10 feet
C. 5 feet
D. 20 feet

44. Where a metal fence is located WITHIN_____ horizontally of the inside walls of a swimming pool, it is required to be bonded to the reinforcing steel of the pool structure, unless separated from the pool by a permanent barrier.

A. 5 feet
B. 6 feet
C. 10 feet
D. 20 feet

45. For permanently installed swimming pools, pool-associated motors shall be connected to an equipment grounding conductor NOT smaller than size _____.

A. 14 AWG
B. 12 AWG
C. 10 AWG
D. 8 AWG

46. Any electric sign installed within a fountain shall be at LEAST_____ inside the fountain, measured from the outside edges of the fountain.

A. 1½ feet
B. 2 feet
C. 5 feet
D. 6 feet

47. Where underground installed rigid PVC conduit, without concrete encasement, is located less than 5 feet from the inside wall of a pool, the conduit must be provided with an earth cover of NOT less than _____.

A. 2 feet
B. 6 inches
C. 18 inches
D. 12 inches

48. All electric swimming pool water heaters shall have the heating elements subdivided into loads not exceeding 48 amperes and protected at NOT over _____.

A. 45 amperes
B. 50 amperes
C. 55 amperes
D. 60 amperes

49. In regard to new outdoor installations of permanently installed swimming pools, luminaries installed above the pool or within 5 feet horizontally from the inside wall of the pool, shall be installed at a height NOT less than _____ above the maximum water level of the pool.

A. 10 feet
B. 12 feet
C. 15 feet
D. 8 feet

50. Where an outdoor installed listed packaged spa or hot tub is provided with cord-and-plug connections, the flexible cord shall NOT be longer than _____ where protected with a ground-fault circuit interrupter.

A. 15 feet
B. 10 feet
C. 6 feet
D. 20 feet

END OF UNIT FIFTEEN

UNIT SIXTEEN

NEC® QUESTIONS FROM ARTICLE 682 THROUGH ARTICLE 725

The following National Electrical Code® questions are typical of questions encountered on all electricians' exams, based on the above referenced Articles of the Code. Select the best answer from the choices given then review your answers with the answer key at the back of this book.

ARTICLE 682 – NATURAL and ARTIFICIALLY MADE BODIES of WATER
****

1. In regard to artificially made bodies of water, liquidtight flexible metal conduit (LFMC) is a wiring method permitted for use for a feeder or branch-circuit where flexibility is required; which of the following listed wiring methods is also approved for this use?

A. UF cable
B. TC cable
C. USE cable
D. extra-hard usage potable power cable

2. When water reaches the height of the established electrical datum plane for an irrigation pond, the service equipment must _____.

A. be installed in a NEMA 6 enclosure
B. float
C. be installed in a NEMA 6P enclosure
D. disconnect

3. Where GFCI protected 125-volt, 15- and 20-ampere receptacles are located outdoors in or on floating buildings or structures within a water treatment facility, the GFCI protection device shall be located NOT less than _____ above the established electrical datum plane.

A. 12 inches
B. 18 inches
C. 24 inches
D. 36 inches

4. The equipotential plane about artificially made bodies of water is necessary to prevent a difference in _____ from developing with in the plane.

A. wattage
B. current
C. voltage
D. resistance

5. Equipotential planes about artificially made bodies of water are required to be bonded to the electrical grounding system by means of a solid insulated or bare copper conductor NOT smaller than _____.

A. 6 AWG
B. 8 AWG
C. 4 AWG
D. 10 AWG

6. The equipotential planes of natural and artificially made bodies of water shall be installed adjacent to all outdoor metal service equipment or disconnecting means, in or on water and accessible to personnel. The equipotential plane shall encompass the area around the equipment and shall extend from the area directly below the equipment out NOT less than _____ in all directions.

A. 24 inches
B. 36 inches
C. 48 inches
D. 60 inches

ARTICLE 690 - SOLAR PHOTOVOLTAIC SYSTEMS
****

7. Solar photovoltaic systems in one- and two-family dwellings with output circuits OVER_____ to ground shall not be accessible to unqualified persons while energized.

A. 50 volts
B. 100 volts
C. 150 volts
D. 200 volts

8. Storage batteries in solar photovoltaic systems installed for dwellings shall have the cells connected so as to operate at LESS than _____.

A. 24 volts
B. 50 volts
C. 100 volts
D. 120 volts

9. The output of a utility-interactive inverter of a solar photovoltaic system shall be permitted to be connected to the _____ of the service disconnecting means.

   I. load side
   II. supply side

A. I only
B. II only
C. either I or II
D. neither I nor II

10. Disregarding exceptions, a photovoltaic power source having one conductor of a two-wire system rated OVER _____, and a neutral of a 3-wire system shall be solidly grounded.

A. 24 volts
B. 50 volts
C. 100 volts
D. 120 volts

11. Photovoltaic source circuits and photovoltaic output circuits shall not be contained in the same junction box UNLESS_____.

A. the source circuit conductors have an insulation rating of not less than 600 volts
B. the output circuit conductors have an insulation rating of not less than 600 volts
C. the source circuit conductors have an insulation temperature rating of not less than 120° C
D. unless the conductors of the different systems are separated by a partition

12. For solar photovoltaic source circuits, the MAXIMUM current shall be the sum of parallel module rated short-circuit currents multiplied by _____.

A. 115 percent
B. 125 percent
C. 150 percent
D. 175 percent

13. Where fuses or circuit breakers are used to protect any dc portion of a photovoltaic power system, they shall be marked indicating the appropriate _____.

A. voltage, current, and interrupting ratings
B. voltage, current and cut-off ratings
C. voltage, current and cut-out ratings
D. voltage, cut-off and disconnect ratings

14. Where photovoltaic source and output circuits operating at maximum system voltages GREATER than _____ are installed in readily accessible locations, circuit conductors shall be installed in a raceway.

A. 24 volts
B. 30 volts
C. 50 volts
D. 12 volts

15. Single-conductor cable Type _____ shall be permitted in exposed outdoor locations in photovoltaic source circuits for photovoltaic module interconnections within the photovoltaic array.

A. UF
B. THHN
C. USE-2
D. THWN

16. In regard to the connectors provided for a module of a photovoltaic system, the grounding member shall be the _____ contact with the mating connector.

A. first to make and last to break
B. first to make and first to break
C. last to make and first to break
D. last to make and last to break

17. For solar photovoltaic systems, locating the system grounding connection point as close as practical to the photovoltaic source better protects the system from _____.

A. excessive voltage drop
B. excessive resistance in the grounding system
C. voltage surges due to lighting
D. voltage surges due to ground-faults

18. For solar photovoltaic systems, all interactive system(s) points of interconnection with other sources shall be marked at an accessible location at the disconnecting means as a power source and with the rated ac output current and the _____.

A. rated ac input current
B. nominal operating ac voltage
C. nominal operating dc voltage
D. rated dc input current

19. A photovoltaic power source for a dwelling shall be permitted to be connected to the load side of the service disconnect of the other source, provided that the sum of the ampere ratings of overcurrent devices supplying power to a busbar or conductor does NOT exceed _____ of the busbar rating.

A. 130 percent
B. 120 percent
C. 110 percent
D. 100 percent

ARTICLE 695 – FIRE PUMPS
****

20. Conductors between the controller and the diesel engine of a fire-pump are required by the NEC® to be _____.

A. 90° C rated
B. 104° C rated
C. stranded
D. solid

21. All energized parts of fire pump equipment shall be located at LEAST _____ above the floor level.

A. 6 feet
B. 5 feet
C. 3 feet
D. 1 foot

22. When sizing the overcurrent protective device(s) for fire pumps, they shall be selected to set or carry indefinitely the sum of the _____ of the fire pump motor(s) and the fire pump associated equipment.

A. locked-rotor current
B. full-load running current
C. nameplate rating
D. starting current

23. Conductors supplying a fire pump motor shall have overload protection set at NOT more than _____ of the full-load running current of the motor.

A. 115 percent
B. 130 percent
C. 140 percent
D. None of these apply, because fire pump motors shall not have automatic protection against overloads.

24. In general, the voltage at the motor terminals of a fire pump shall NOT drop more than _____ below the voltage rating of the motor when the motor is operating at 115 percent of the full-load current rating of the motor.

A. 3 percent
B. 5 percent
C. 2 percent
D. 15 percent

ARTICLE 700 - EMERGENCY SYSTEMS
****

25. All boxes and enclosures for emergency system circuits shall be _____.

A. permanently marked and readily identified
B. locked in the open position
C. permanently sealed
D. readily accessible

26. When installing emergency battery pack lighting equipment, such as exit luminaries, the branch-circuit supplying this equipment shall _____.

A. be connected to the nearest receptacle outlet
B. come from the closest outlet of power that is compatible with the rated voltage of the emergency luminaire
C. be fed only from an identified emergency lighting panelboard
D. be on the same branch-circuit serving the normal lighting in the area

27. Feeder-circuit wiring for emergency systems shall be installed in spaces or areas that are fully protected by an approved automatic fire suppression system or protected by a listed fire-rated assembly that has a MINIMUM fire rating of _____.

A. 2 hours
B. 3 hours
C. 1 hour
D. 4 hours

28. Upon the loss of normal power, storage batteries used as a source of power for emergency systems shall be of suitable rating and capacity to supply and maintain the total load for a MINIMUM period of _____ without the voltage applied to the load falling below 87½ percent of normal.

A. 3/4 hour
B. 1 hour
C. 1½ hours
D. 2 hours

29. Emergency lighting circuits are not permitted to be controlled by _____.

A. single-throw switches
B. fused switches
C. switches connected in parallel
D. three-way and four-way switches

30. A source of power for an emergency system to a building may be _____.

A. a storage battery
B. a generator set
C. a separate service
D. any of these

31. Where practical, audible and visual signal devices for an emergency system shall be provided to indicate _____.

   I. the battery is carrying a load
   II. the battery charger is not functioning

A. I only
B. II only
C. neither I nor II
D. both I and II

32. Where internal combustion engines are used as the prime-mover for an emergency system, an on-site fuel supply shall be provided sufficient for NOT less than _____ full-demand operation of the system.

A. 1 hour
B. 1½ hours
C. 2 hours
D. 2½ hours

33. When generators are used as a source of supply for emergency systems, in the event of failure of the normal electrical supply to the building, the generator shall have a starting time NOT to exceed _____, unless an auxiliary power supply will energize the emergency system until the generator can pick up the load.

A. 10 seconds
B. 20 seconds
C. 30 seconds
D. 60 seconds

34. In regard to emergency and legally required standby systems, transfer switches shall be _____ and approved by the authority having jurisdiction.

A. manual
B. automatic
C. non-automatic
D. red in color

35. Which of the following types of batteries is NOT acceptable for use as a source of power for emergency systems?

A. sealed
B. lead acid
C. automotive
D. transparent

ARTICLE 701 – LEGALLY REQUIRED STANDBY SYSTEMS
****

36. The branch-circuit overcurrent devices in legally required standby circuits shall be accessible to _____ only.

A. management personnel
B. qualified persons
C. authorized persons
D. the local authority having jurisdiction

37. Storage batteries for legally required standby systems shall have the capacity to maintain not less than 87½ percent of the system voltage of the circuits supplying the legally required standby power for a period of at LEAST _____, upon loss of the normal power.

A. 1 hour
B. 1 ½ hours
C. 2 hours
D. 3 hours

38. For municipal buildings having legally required standby systems, in the event of failure of the normal power supply, the legally required standby system is mandated to automatically supply power to selected loads within at LEAST _____.

A. 60 seconds
B. 10 seconds
C. 45 seconds
D. 5 minutes

39. Unit equipment, such as emergency lighting, supplied by legally required standby systems is permitted to be cord-and-plug connected provided the cord does NOT exceed _____ in length.

A. 12 inches
B. 18 inches
C. 24 inches
D. 36 inches

ARTICLE 702 – OPTIONAL STANDBY SYSTEMS
****

40. Transfer equipment of optional standby systems shall be suitable for the intended use and design, and installed so as to prevent the inadvertent interconnection of _____ sources of supply in any operation of the transfer equipment.

A. ac and dc
B. primary and secondary
C. input and output
D. normal and alternate

41. Optional standby systems are intended to supply on-site generated power to selected loads _____.

A. manually only
B. automatically only
C. either automatically or manually
D. by means of a separate service

ARTICLE 725 - CLASS 1, CLASS 2, and CLASS 3 REMOTE-CONTROL, SIGNALING, and POWER-LIMITED CIRCUITS
****

42. Class 1 power-limited circuits shall be supplied from a source that has a rated output of NOT more than _____.

A. 24 volts and 1250 volt-amperes
B. 30 volts and 1000 volt-amperes
C. 50 volts and 1000 volt-amperes
D. 30 volts and 1250 volt-amperes

43. Overcurrent protection for size 16 AWG conductors for Class 1 circuits shall NOT exceed _____.

A. 5 amperes
B. 7 amperes
C. 10 amperes
D. 12 amperes

44. Class 1, Class 2, and Class 3 circuits shall be installed in a _____ manner.

A. neat and workmanlike
B. functional and neat
C. neat and appealing
D. safe and neat

45. Where only Class 1 circuit conductors are in a raceway, the derating factors given in Section 310.15(B)(3)(a) of the NEC® shall apply ONLY if the conductors _____.

A. have an insulation rating of 60° C
B. do not have an insulation rating of 90° C
C. are of a size 14 AWG or less
D. carry continuous loads in excess of 10 percent of the ampacity of each conductor

46. Class 1 circuits and power supply circuits shall be permitted to occupy the same raceway or enclosure _____.

A. never
B. where the Class 1 circuit conductors are of size 12 AWG and larger
C. where the equipment powered is not functionally associated
D. only where the equipment powered is functionally associated

47. In hoistways, Class 2 or Class 3 circuit conductors shall NOT be installed in _____.

A. electrical metallic tubing
B. rigid nonmetallic conduit
C. electrical nonmetallic tubing
D. intermediate metal conduit

48. Class 2 cables shall have a voltage rating of NOT less than _____.

A. 150 volts
B. 250 volts
C. 300 volts
D. 600 volts

49. Which of the following listed cables is approved for installations in ducts, plenums, and other spaces used for environmental air?

A. CL3X
B. CL3
C. CMR
D. CL3P

50. Conductors of Class 2 circuits shall be permitted within the same raceway with conductors of Class 3 circuits provided _____.

A. the insulation of the Class 3 circuits is equal to the insulation of the Class 2 circuits
B. the insulation of the Class 2 circuits is equal to the insulations of the Class 3 circuits
C. the applied voltage of the Class 3 circuits is not more than 24 volts
D. the conductors are installed in nonmetallic raceways

END OF UNIT SIXTEEN
****

UNIT SEVENTEEN

NEC® QUESTIONS FROM ARTICLE 760 THROUGH APPENDIX C

The following National Electrical Code® questions are typical of questions encountered on all electricians' exams, based on the above referenced Articles of the Code. Select the best answer from the choices given then review your answers with the answer key at the back of this book.

ARTICLE 760 - FIRE ALARM SYSTEMS
****

1. In hoistways, power-limited fire alarm (PLFA) circuit cables shall NOT be installed in _____.

A. electrical metallic tubing
B. rigid nonmetallic conduit
C. intermediate metal conduit
D. electrical nonmetallic tubing

2. Non-power-limited fire alarm (NPLFA) signaling circuit conductors shall be _____.

A. copper
B. aluminum
C. red in color
D. orange in color

3. What is the MAXIMUM allowable overcurrent protection for size 16 AWG conductors in a non-power-limited fire alarm (NPLFA) signaling circuit?

A. 7 amperes
B. 8 amperes
C. 10 amperes
D. 12 amperes

4. The derating factors given in Section 310.15(B)(3)(a) of the NEC® do not apply to NPLFA circuits if the conductors are loaded to LESS than _____ continuously.

A. 10 percent
B. 25 percent
C. 75 percent
D. 80 percent

5. Multiconductor NPLFA cables shall be permitted to be used on fire alarm circuits operating at a MAXIMUM of _____.

A. 120 volts
B. 150 volts
C. 24 volts
D. 50 volts

6. Where multiconductor NPLFA cables are located within 7 feet of the floor, the cables shall be fastened in an approved manner at intervals of NOT more than _____.

A. 18 inches
B. 2 feet
C. 2½ feet
D. 4½ feet

7. NPLFA circuit conductors are permitted to be installed in the same raceway with_____.

   I. Class 1 conductors
   II. power supply conductors

A. I only
B. II only
C. both I and II
D. neither I nor II

8. Coaxial cables used in power-limited fire alarm (PLFA) systems shall be listed as Type:

   I. FPLR
   II. CXPL

A. I only
B. II only
C. either I or II
D. neither I nor II

9. Type FPLA fire alarm cables installed within buildings shall be listed as being resistant to the spread of fire and have a voltage rating of NOT less than _____.

A. 150 volts
B. 250 volts
C. 300 volts
D. 600 volts

10. Where multiconductor non-power-limited fire alarm (NPLFA) circuit conductors pass through a wall, the conductors shall be protected by a metal raceway or rigid nonmetallic conduit up to a height of at LEAST _____ above the floor, unless other means of protection is provided.

A. 8 feet
B. 6 feet
C. 7 feet
D. 10 feet

11. Splices in power-limited fire alarm (PLFA) circuit conductors are permitted to be made _____.

A. in sealed ceiling spaces
B. exposed without protection
C. within enclosed walls
D. in junction boxes

12. Branch-circuit conductors supplying fire alarm circuits are permitted to be supplied through _____.

   I. ground-fault circuit interrupters
   II. arc-fault circuit interrupters

A. I only
B. II only
C. either I or II
D. neither I nor II

13. Openings around penetrations of fire alarm cables and raceways through fire-resistant rated walls shall be _____.

A. fireproofed
B. firestopped
C. soundproofed
D. sleeved

14. In general, transformers supplied from power-limited fire alarm (PLFA) circuits shall be protected with an overcurrent device rated NOT over _____.

A. 7 amperes
B. 10 amperes
C. 15 amperes
D. 20 amperes

15. Where power-limited fire alarm (PLFA) circuits are installed in a fire alarm control panel (FACP) with non-power-limited fire alarm (NPLFA) and power circuits, the power-limited circuit conductors are required to have a separation of NOT less than _____ from the other circuit conductors.

A. 1/4 in.
B. 1/2 in.
C. 3/4 in.
D. 1 in.

16. The accessible portion of abandoned fire alarm cables shall be _____.

A. identified with a red colored tag
B. identified with an orange colored tag
C. removed
D. protected by a metal raceway

17. NPLFA cables used in a wet location shall be listed for use in wet locations or have _____.

A. a nylon outer covering
B. THHN insulation
C. a moisture-impervious nonmetallic sheath
D. a moisture-impervious metal sheath

18. Insulated conductors of non-power limited fire alarm (NPLFA) cables installed within buildings shall be suitable for _____.

A. 150 volts
B. 250 volts
C. 300 volts
D. 600 volts

ARTICLE 770 – OPTICAL FIBER CABLES and RACEWAYS
****

19. Nonconductive optical fiber cable may occupy the same raceway with conductors supplying luminaires and power, provided the operating voltage does NOT exceed _____.

A. 120 volts
B. 250 volts
C. 480 volts
D. 600 volts

20. Which of the following listed is NOT a type of optical fiber cable?

A. composite
B. non-composite
C. conductive
D. non-conductive

21. The primary protector grounding terminal of optical fiber cables shall be bonded to the metal frame or available grounding terminal of a mobile home with a copper grounding conductor NOT smaller than _____ where the mobile home is supplied by cord-and-plug connections.

A. 6 AWG
B. 8 AWG
C. 12 AWG
D. 10 AWG

ARTICLE 800 - COMMUNICATIONS CIRCUITS

22. Where communications cables are installed in plenums or in spaces used for environmental air, they shall be listed as _____.

A. Type CMP
B. Type CMR
C. Type MPB
D. Type MPR

23. Disregarding exceptions, communications wires and cables above roofs shall have a vertical clearance of at LEAST how many feet from all points of roofs above which they pass?

A. 3 feet
B. 4 feet
C. 6 feet
D. 8 feet

24. In general, communications wires and cables shall be separated at LEAST _____ from electric light and power conductors.

A. 2 inches
B. 4 inches
C. 6 inches
D. 8 inches

25. Where practical, a separation of at LEAST _____ shall be maintained between communications wires and cables on buildings and lightning conductors.

A. 6 feet
B. 10 feet
C. 3 feet
D. 4 feet

26. Where a telephone cable is to be installed through a fire-resistant-rated wall in a home to a telephone in an attached garage, in order to be in compliance with the NEC®, what provisions must be made?

A. Junction boxes must be installed on both sides of the wall, connected with a conduit nipple.
B. Openings around the penetration must be firestopped using approved methods.
C. No penetrations of any kind may be made through a fire-resistant-rated wall.
D. None of the above.

27. A bonding jumper NOT smaller than _____ copper shall be connected between the communications grounding electrode and the power grounding electrode system at the building or structure served, where separate electrodes are used.

A. 12 AWG
B. 10 AWG
C. 8 AWG
D. 6 AWG

28. Overhead communications wires and cables shall have a MINUMUM separation of _____ from supply service drops of 0-750 volts at any point in the span.

A. 30 inches
B. 24 inches
C. 12 inches
D. 18 inches

29. Underground communications wires and cables are permitted in a manhole containing electric light and power conductors where _____.

A. the communications wires and cables are in nonmetallic raceways
B. the communications wires and cables are in metallic raceways
C. the electric light and power conductors are enclosed in separate raceways
D. the communications wires and cables are in a section separated from the other conductors by means of a suitable barrier

30. On buildings, communications wires and cables shall be separated at LEAST _____ from power conductors not in a raceway.

A. 4 inches
B. 6 inches
C. 12 inches
D. 18 inches

31. For communications wires and cables, where there exists a probability of exposure to lightning, each interbuilding communications circuit on a premise shall be protected by _____.

A. a primary protector at each end of the interbuilding circuit
B. a secondary protector at each end of the interbuilding circuit
C. a metal conduit throughout the building
D. a nonmetallic conduit throughout the building

32. Interbuilding communications circuits are not considered to have a lightning exposure when the interbuilding cable runs are ran between two buildings and the cable runs are of _____ or less, directly buried, or in an underground conduit and connected to each building grounding electrode system.

A. 50 feet
B. 100 feet
C. 140 feet
D. 150 feet

33. The metal grounding conductor sheath of communications cables shall NOT be smaller than _____, where it enters a building.

A. 16 AWG
B. 14 AWG
C. 12 AWG
D. 10 AWG

34. Communications wires and cables shall have a voltage rating of NOT less than_____.

A. 60 volts
B. 120 volts
C. 300 volts
D. 600 volts

ARTICLE 810 - RADIO and TELEVISION EQUIPMENT

35. What is the MINIMUM size protective bonding or grounding electrode conductor permitted for an amateur radio-TV transmitting station?

A. 8 AWG
B. 10 AWG
C. 12 AWG
D. 14 AWG

36. Outdoor antenna conductors of hard-drawn copper, for receiving stations, shall be a MINIMUM size of _____, if the open span length is over 150 feet.

A. 12 AWG
B. 14 AWG
C. 17 AWG
D. 19 AWG

37. Outdoor antenna conductors for amateur and citizen band transmitting and receiving stations shall be a MINIMUM size of _____ hard-drawn copper.

A. 10 AWG
B. 12 AWG
C. 14 AWG
D. 20 AWG

ARTICLE 820 - COMMUNITY ANTENNA TELEVISION and RADIO DISTRIBUTION SYSTEMS

38. Where power for equipment that is directly associated with the radio frequency distribution system is carried by the coaxial cable, and the power source is a power limiting transformer, what is the MAXIMUM voltage this coaxial cable may carry?

A. 50 volts
B. 60 volts
C. 120 volts
D. 150 volts

39. Where practical, coaxial cables for a CATV system shall be separated from lightning conductors of at LEAST _____.

A. 2 feet
B. 2½ feet
C. 4 feet
D. 6 feet

CHAPTER 9 - TABLES
****

40. Where conduit or tubing nipples having a MAXIMUM length NOT to exceed _____ are installed between boxes or similar enclosures, the nipples shall be permitted to be filled to 60 percent of their total cross-sectional area.

A. 24 inches
B. 26 inches
C. 30 inches
D. 36 inches

41. Where a 36 in. long conduit contains one (1) ungrounded conductor, one (1) grounded conductor and one (1) equipment grounding conductor, the conduit may be filled to a MAXIMUM of _____ its cross-sectional area.

A. 53 percent
B. 31 percent
C. 40 percent
D. 60 percent

42. The internal total area, in square inches, of trade size 2 in. electrical metallic tubing (EMT) is _____.

A. 2.067 sq. in.
B. 3.356 sq. in.
C. 1.342 sq. in.
D. 1.040 sq. in.

43. Where a combination of more than two conductors having a total area of 2.01 sq. inches are to be installed in a 30 ft. long rigid metal conduit (RMC), what is the MINIMUM standard trade size conduit the NEC® requires for this installation?

A. 2 in.
B. 2½ in.
C. 3 in.
D. 3½ in.

44. The approximate area, in square inches, of a size 4 AWG RHW-2 conductor without outer covering is _____ .

A. 0.1333 sq. in.
B. 0.412 sq. in.
C. 0.352 sq. in.
D. 0.0973 sq. in.

45. The circular mil area of a size 2 AWG copper conductor is _____.

A. 66,360 circular mils
B. 133,100 circular mils
C. 52,620 circular mils
D. 41,740 circular mils

46. Where a trade size 2 in. rigid metal conduit (RMC) is field bent with a full-shoe or one-shot conduit bender, the radius of the curve of the bend to the centerline of the conduit shall NOT be less than _____.

A. 12 inches
B. 9 ½ inches
C. 8 ¼ inches
D. 10 ½ inches

47. For the purposes of determining conductor fill in conduit, a flexible cord or cable of four (4) conductors shall be treated as _____ conductor(s).

A. one
B. two
C. three
D. four

48. For cables that have elliptical cross sections, the cross-sectional area calculation shall be based on using the _____ of the ellipse as a circular diameter.

A. major diameter
B. minor diameter
C. total diameter
D. circular diameter

APPENDIX C - CONDUIT and TUBING FILL TABLES for CONDUCTORS of the SAME SIZE
****

49. The NEC® permits no more than _____ size 3 AWG XHHW-2 aluminum conductors to be installed in a trade size 2½ in. Schedule 40 rigid PVC conduit having a length of more than 2 feet.

A. fourteen
B. thirteen
C. nineteen
D. sixteen

50. What is the MAXIMUM number of size 12 AWG THWN copper conductors that may be installed in a trade size 1 in. electrical metallic tubing (EMT) having a length of 50 feet?

A. 16
B. 26
C. 45
D. 13

END OF UNIT SEVENTEEN
****

NOTES

UNIT EIGHTEEN
FINAL EXAM # 1

RANDOM QUESTIONS THROUGHOUT THE NEC®.

This is an "OPEN BOOK" practice electricians' exam. A 2011 edition of the NATIONAL ELECTRICAL CODE is the only reference that should be used on this exam. This practice exam is typical of questions encountered on all electricians' exams. Select the best answer from the choices given then review your answers with the answer key at the back of this book.

ALLOTED TIME: 2½ hours

1. The NEC® considers an electric water heater to be _____.

   I. an appliance
   II. utilization equipment

A. I only
B. II only
C. both I and II
D. neither I nor II

2. The space under raised floors of computer rooms where air ducts are connected and that forms part of the air distribution system is known as a/an_____.

A. crawl space
B. air duct space
C. plenum
D. dedicated electrical space

3. Service conductors shall be considered outside a building where _____.

   I. installed within the building, in a raceway that is encased in concrete less than 2 inches thick
   II. installed in a transformer vault

A. I only
B. II only
C. both I and II
D. neither I nor II

4. Service conductors supplying a building are permitted to pass through the interior of another building if _____.

   I. the conductors are installed in metal conduit
   II. the conductors pass through the attic of the other building

A. I only
B. II only
C. both I and II
D. neither I nor II

5. What is the MINIMUM distance required between a warning ribbon and underground service lateral conductors?

A. 6 inches
B. 12 inches
C. 18 inches
D. 24 inches

6. The NEC® mandates the MAXIMUM length of an equipment bonding jumper when installed outside of a raceway to be _____.

A. 3 feet
B. 6 feet
C. 9 feet
D. 12 feet

7. For other than one-family dwellings, what is the MINIMUM size overhead service conductors required where supplying a building or structure having only six (6) 20-ampere, 120-volt, single-phase branch-circuits?

A. 8 AWG aluminum
B. 6 AWG copper
C. 8 AWG copper
D. 4 AWG aluminum

8. All metallic switchgear rated over 600 volts shall be provided with a grounding busbar for the purposes of connecting the _____.

A. grounded conductors
B. metallic shield of cables
C. metal raceways
D. ungrounded conductors

9. Rod and pipe grounding electrodes shall be permitted to be buried in a trench _____.

A. under all circumstances
B. under no circumstances
C. that has a depth of 2 feet
D. when rock bottom is encountered

10. Which one of the following listed conductor insulation types is flame-retardant and moisture resistant thermoset?

A. TW
B. TFE
C. RHW
D. RUH

11. Transfer equipment of optional standby systems shall be suitable for the intended use and design and installed so as to prevent the inadvertent interconnection of _____ sources of supply in any operation of the transfer equipment.

A. ac and dc
B. primary and secondary
C. input and output
D. normal and alternate

12. In general, what is the SMALLEST size grounded or ungrounded conductor permitted to be connected in parallel?

A. 1/0 AWG
B. 1 AWG
C. 2 AWG
D. 10 AWG

13. A receptacle outlet installed to serve a kitchen countertop space may be located a MAXIMUM of how many inches above the countertop?

A. 12 inches
B. 18 inches
C. 20 inches
D. 24 inches

14. In general, the MAXIMUM height above the floor of the operating handle of a standard main disconnect switch, when it is in the *ON* position must NOT exceed _____.

A. 5½ ft.
B. 6 ft.
C. 6 ½ ft.
D. 6 ft.-7 in.

15. Where buried raceways pass under a public driveway, the MINIMUM cover requirements _____.

A. decrease if installed in rigid metal conduit (RMC)
B. do not change in regard to wiring methods used
C. shall be increased for direct buried cables
D. can be increased, decreased or remain the same, depending on the wiring method

16. Where there are two (2) internal cable clamps in a metal box, the number of conductors allowed in the box shall be reduced by _____.

A. none
B. one
C. two
D. three

17. What is the MINIMUM separation required between thermal insulation and a recessed luminaire enclosure, unless it is identified as Type IC, approved for contact with insulation?

A. 1/2 inch
B. 2 inches
C. 3 inches
D. 4 inches

18. When trade size 3/8 in. flexible metal conduit (FMC) is used as a *fixture whip* from an outlet box to a luminaire, the FMC shall NOT exceed _____ in length.

A. 4 feet
B. 5 feet
C. 6 feet
D. 10 feet

19. Each luminaire installed in Class III, Divisions 1 and 2 locations shall be clearly marked to show the maximum wattage of the lamps that shall be permitted without exceeding an exposed surface temperature of _____ under normal conditions of use.

A. 329° F
B. 165° F
C. 144° F
D. 125° F

20. Busways shall be securely supported at intervals NOT exceeding _____ unless otherwise designed and marked.

A. 6 feet
B. 5 feet
C. 10 feet
D. 12 feet

21. How many 125-volt, 15- or 20-ampere rated receptacle outlets are required to be readily accessible in guest rooms or guest suites of motels and hotels after the furniture is placed?

A. one
B. two
C. three
D. four

22. The NEC® mandates the MINIMUM size conductor for integrated gas spacer cable (Type IGS) to be _____.

A. 2 AWG
B. 1/0 AWG
C. 4/0 AWG
D. 250 kcmil

23. In Class II, Division 1 hazardous locations, an approved method of connection of conduit to boxes is _____.

A. compression fittings
B. threaded bosses
C. welding
D. none of these

24. The bonding conductor associated with hydromassage bathtubs shall be connected to the _____.

A. grounding electrode
B. branch-circuit panelboard
C. service equipment
D. terminal on the circulating pump motor that is intended for this purpose

25. A 125-volt, single-phase, receptacle provided for the servicing of rooftop located HVAC equipment shall be located within 25 feet of the equipment and be _____.

A. supplied from a dedicated 20 ampere circuit
B. on the same level as the equipment
C. connected to the load side of the equipment disconnect
D. connected to the line side of the equipment disconnect

26. When NM cable is installed through slots or holes in metal framing member, the NEC® required which of the following for the protection of the cable?

A. Listed bushings or grommets installed after cable installation.
B. Listed bushings or grommets installed before cable installation.
C. Split bushings or grommets installed after cable installation.
D. The NEC® permits any of these installations.

27. The required size of the equipment bonding jumper and the main bonding jumper on the supply side of the building service is based on the size of the _____.

A. service-entrance conductors
B. feeder conductors
C. overcurrent device
D. fault-current

28. The branch-circuit overcurrent device shall be permitted to serve as the disconnecting means for stationary motors rated NOT greater than _____.

A. 2 hp
B. 1 hp
C. 1/2 hp
D. 1/8 hp

29. A device that provides a means for connecting communications system(s) bonding conductor(s) to the grounding electrode system at the service equipment or at the disconnecting means for buildings, is defined in the NEC® as a/an _____.

A. intersystem grounding electrode
B. intersystem bonding termination
C. communications grounding termination
D. communications grounding electrode

30. Electrically heated floors of bathrooms, hydromassage bathtub, spa, and hot tub locations shall be _____.

A. GFCI protected
B. isolated
C. grounded
D. bonded

31. Circuit breakers used as switches for 120 volt and 277 volt fluorescent lighting branch-circuits, shall be listed for the purpose and shall be _____.

A. marked "SWD"
B. bolt in style breakers only
C. bolt in style breakers and marked "SWD"
D. marked "FLS"

32. In general, a generator that does not require overcurrent protection is a _____.

A. two wire generator
B. constant voltage generator
C. generator operating at 65 volts or less
D. three wire, direct current generator

33. Single-conductor supply conductors to a portable switchboard located on a theatrical stage shall NOT be smaller than _____.

A. 8 AWG
B. 6 AWG
C. 4 AWG
D. 2 AWG

34. The area within 3 feet of the open end of a vent discharging upward from an underground gasoline tank at a service station shall be classified as _____.

A. Class I, Division 1
B. Class I, Division 2
C. Class II, Division 1
D. Class II, Division 2

35. For Class I, Division 2 locations in industrial establishments with restricted public access where the conditions of maintenance and supervision ensure that only qualified persons service the installation and where metallic conduit does not provide sufficient corrosion resistance, _____ shall be permitted.

A. Schedule 40 PVC conduit
B. flexible nonmetallic conduit
C. flexible nonmetallic tubing
D. RTRC with the suffix -XW

36. A phase converter is an electrical device that converts _____.

A. ac voltage to dc voltage
B. 3-phase power to single-phase power
C. single-phase power to 3-phase power
D. ungrounded systems to grounded systems

37. When multiple driven ground rods are installed, the MINIMUM required distance between the rod electrodes to keep the resistance to ground 25 ohms or less is _____.

A. 5 feet
B. 6 feet
C. 8 feet
D. 10 feet

38. Disregarding exceptions, where a motor of more than 1 horsepower has a temperature rise of 50° C indicated on the nameplate, for the purpose of selecting the overload device, this device shall be selected to trip at NO more than _____ of the motor's full-load ampere rating indicated on the motor nameplate.

A. 100 percent
B. 115 percent
C. 125 percent
D. 130 percent

39. A fire alarm pull station shall NOT be less than _____ from the inside walls of a permanently installed swimming pool.

A. 10 feet
B. 15 feet
C. 20 feet
D. 25 feet

40. Where nails are used as a fastening means for device boxes and they pass through the interior of the box _____.

A. the nails are required to be galvanized
B. the box shall not be less than 2 in. deep
C. the nails shall be within ¼ in. of the back or end of the box
D. the NEC® prohibits this installation

41. Where a manufacturing plant makes aluminum brake pads in an area containing combustible aluminum metal dust, this area is considered to be a Class II, _____ hazardous location.

A. Group C
B. Group D
C. Group E
D. Group F

42. Branch-circuit conductors within three (3) inches of a ballast, inside a ballast compartment, shall have an insulation rating NOT lower than _____.

A. 105° C
B. 90° C
C. 75° C
D. 60° C

43. Which of the following listed shall be connected to the life safety branch of the emergency system of a health care facility?

A. kitchen equipment
B. automatic operated doors used for building egress
C. electrical equipment rooms
D. doctors' offices

44. When ungrounded conductors are adjusted in size to compensate for voltage drop, equipment grounding conductors, where installed, shall be adjusted proportionately according to the _____ of the ungrounded conductors.

A. diameter in inches
B. area in square inches
C. circular mil area
D. temperature rating

45. When calculating the general lighting load for a dwelling unit, which of the following listed is NOT required to be included in the calculation?

A. hallways
B. bathrooms
C. clothes closets
D. open porches

46. Where a conduit contains only two (2) conductors, it may be filled to a MAXIMUM of _____ of its cross-sectional area.

A. 53 percent
B. 31 percent
C. 40 percent
D. 60 percent

47. For the purpose of determining conductor fill in a device box, the NEC® mandates a 3-way switch is to be counted as equal to two (2) conductors. The volume allowance for the two (2) conductors shall be based on _____.

A. the largest conductor in the box
B. the largest grounding conductor in the box
C. the number of clamps in the box
D. the largest conductor connected to the switch

48. The reason the NEC® requires each separate phase conductor of an electrical system to be located in the same ferrous metal raceway is to _____.

A. reduce inductive heat
B. provide identification of a circuit
C. assure balanced resistance
D. improve workmanship

49. Where abandoned communications cables are identified for future use with a tag, the tag shall be _____.

A. red in color
B. orange in color
C. located outside the junction box
D. of sufficient durability to withstand the environment

50. For nonshielded conductors of over 600 volts, the conductor shall not be bent to a radius of LESS than _____ times the overall conductor diameter.

A. six
B. eight
C. ten
D. twelve

END OF UNIT EIGHTEEN

NOTES

UNIT NINETEEN
FINAL EXAM # 2

RANDOM QUESTIONS THROUGHOUT THE NEC®.

This is an "OPEN BOOK" practice electricians' exam. A 2011 edition of the NATIONAL ELECTRICAL CODE is the only reference that should be used on this exam. This practice exam is typical of questions encountered on all electricians' exams. Select the best answer from the choices given then review your answers with the answer key at the back of this book.

ALLOTED TIME: 2½ hours

1. What is the MAXIMUM distance permitted between supports for straight horizontal runs of trade size 1½ in. threaded rigid metal conduit (RMC)?

A. 10 feet
B. 12 feet
C. 14 feet
D. 16 feet

2. Bends in Type NM cable shall be made so that the radius of the curve of the inner edge of any bend shall NOT be less than _____.

A. five times the diameter of the cable
B. seven times the diameter of the cable
C. seven times the circular mil area of the conductors
D. five times the circular mil area of the conductors

3. A type of an approved grounding electrode is a ground ring encircling the building or structure, in direct contact with the earth for at LEAST _____ consisting of bare copper not smaller than 2 AWG.

A. 10 feet
B. 20 feet
C. 30 feet
D. 50 feet

4. As per the NEC®, a neutral conductor is always _____.

A. a grounded conductor
B. an ungrounded conductor
C. white in color
D. the conductor connected to the neutral point of a system that is intended to carry current under normal conditions

5. Where the opening to an outlet box is less than 8 in. in any dimension, the length of free conductor that must extend from the outside opening of the box is _____.

A. 3 inches
B. 4 inches
C. 5 inches
D. 6 inches

6. For indoor installations about switchboards and panelboards, the space equal to the width and depth of the equipment and extending from the floor to a height of 6 feet above the equipment or to the structural ceiling, is defined as the _____.

A. dedicated electrical space
B. headroom space
C. personnel space
D. equipment clearance space

7. All 125 volt, single-phase receptacle outlets not exceeding 30 amperes and located within at LEAST _____ horizontally of the inside walls of a hydromassage tub are required to be GFCI protected.

A. 5 feet
B. 6 feet
C. 10 feet
D. 15 feet

8. Electric water heaters for swimming pools shall have the heating elements subdivided into loads NOT exceeding _____.

A. 32 amperes
B. 36 amperes
C. 48 amperes
D. 60 amperes

9. Concrete encased raceways approved for burial only, shall require a concrete envelope NOT less than _____ thick.

A. 2 inches
B. 3 inches
C. 4 inches
D. 6 inches

10. An adjustable trip circuit breaker shall be permitted to have an ampere rating that is equal to the adjusted current setting if _____.

A. access is restricted to the adjusting means
B. under 4000 amperes
C. supplying air-conditioning equipment
D. the adjusting means is readily accessible

11. An approved method of protection for equipment installed in Class I, Zone 0, hazardous locations is _____.

A. purged and pressurized
B. encapsulation
C. powder filling
D. oil immersion

12. In locations where batteries are stored, provisions shall be made for ventilation of the gasses from the batteries to prevent _____.

A. corrosion
B. electrolysis
C. electro-magnetic induction
D. the accumulation of an explosive mixture

13. What is the MINIMUM height from final grade for an overhead grounded messenger supported, 120/240 volt, single-phase, service drop to a temporary service pole located on residential property, where there is no truck traffic or driveways?

A. 8 feet
B. 10 feet
C. 12 feet
D. 15 feet

14. The front edge of a switch box installed in a wall constructed of wood or other combustible surface material shall be _____ from the surface of the wall.

A. flush with or projected out
B. set back a maximum of 1/4 in.
C. set back a maximum of 1/2 in.
D. set back a maximum of 3/8 in.

15. A stationary 1½ hp, ac motor may have a general-use snap switch, suitable only for use on ac, for a controller, where _____.

   I. the motor full-load current rating is not more than 80% of the ampere rating of the switch
   II. the motor has a voltage rating of 300 volts or less

A. I only
B. II only
C. both I and II
D. neither I nor II

16. Where a 120-volt, 20-ampere rated single receptacle outlet located in an attached garage of a dwelling unit is provided for a central vacuum assembly, the receptacle outlet is required to have _____.

A. AFCI protection
B. GFCI protection
C. LCDI protection
D. a nonmetallic faceplate

17. In general, what is the largest insulated solid conductor permitted by the NEC® to be pulled into an existing raceway?

A. 4 AWG
B. 6 AWG
C. 8 AWG
D. 10 AWG

18. Which one of the following statements regarding flat conductor cable is TRUE?

A. The cable shall have an current rating not exceeding 20 amperes.
B. The voltage between ungrounded conductors is permitted to exceed 300 volts.
C. Type FCC cable shall be provided with GFCI protection.
D. The cable shall be permitted to be installed on walls in metal raceways.

19. The controller for a torque motor shall have a continuous duty full-load current rating NOT less than _____ of the nameplate current rating of the motor.

A. 100 percent
B. 110 percent
C. 115 percent
D. 125 percent

20. Which one of the following listed wiring methods is approved for use in a duct specifically fabricated to transport environmental air?

A. electrical nonmetallic tubing (ENT)
B. electrical metallic tubing (EMT)
C. Schedule 40 PVC conduit
D. nonmetallic sheathed cable (NM)

21. Determine the MAXIMUM overcurrent protection permitted for size 14 AWG THWN copper motor control circuit conductors tapped from the load side of a motor overcurrent protection device, where the conductors require short-circuit protection and do not extend beyond the motor equipment enclosure.

A. 20 amperes
B. 25 amperes
C. 30 amperes
D. 100 amperes

22. For branch-circuits that supply equipment classed as emergency equipment, there shall be an emergency supply source to which the load will be transferred automatically upon the failure of the _____ supply.

A. back-up
B. generator
C. normal
D. alternate

23. The largest size copper conductor permitted for nonmetallic sheathed cable is size _____.

A. 4 AWG
B. 2 AWG
C. 6 AWG
D. 1 AWG

24. Where a direct-burial cable has a circuit voltage of 45 kV, the NEC® mandates the MINIMUM burial depth of the cable to be _____.

A. 24 inches
B. 36 inches
C. 42 inches
D. 48 inches

25. Conductors, in length up to 25 feet, shall be permitted to be connected to a transformer secondary without overcurrent protection at the secondary if _____.

A. conductors are size 6 AWG copper or larger
B. used in commercial applications only
C. used for industrial installations only
D. the conductors do not penetrate walls, floors, or ceilings

26. What is the MAXIMUM distance permitted for emergency controls from the fuel dispensers at attended self-service gas stations or convenience stores with fuel dispensing facilities?

A. 50 feet
B. 99 feet
C. 100 feet
D. 150 feet

27. Where a service disconnecting means consist of two or three single-pole switches or circuit breakers, capable of individual operation, supplying multiwire circuits, this method of installation is in compliance with the NEC® where _____.

A. devices are listed
B. devices are indicating
C. switches or circuit breakers are linked together using a galvanized nail or other galvanized metal object
D. switches or circuit breakers are equipped with identified handle ties

28. Where a building or structure of a large area is provided with two (2) services, one at each end, _____.

A. each service is required to have a separate grounding electrode
B. only one grounding electrode is permitted
C. the grounding electrodes of each individual service must be isolated from each other
D. the services are required to be connected to a common grounding electrode or the electrodes bonded together

29. Dry type transformers, 600 volts or less, and NOT exceeding _____ shall be permitted in fire-resistant hollow spaces of buildings, such as above an accessible ceiling, where not permanently closed in by structure.

A. 10 kVA
B. 50 kVA
C. 75 kVA
D. 112½ kVA

30. A load where the wave shape of the steady-state current does not follow the wave shape of the applied voltage is defined as _____ in the NEC®.

A. inductive reactance
B. sinusoidal
C. non-sinusoidal
D. nonlinear

31. In dwellings, lighting outlets shall be permitted to be controlled by occupancy sensors provided they are _____.

A. automatic
B. located in the hallway
C. within 6 ft. of door(s)
D. equipped with a manual override

32. Conductors supplying outlets for arc and xenon motion picture projectors of the professional type, shall be a MINIMUM size of _____.

A. 4 AWG
B. 6 AWG
C. 8 AWG
D. 10 AWG

33. Open spaces within 20 feet horizontally and up to 18 inches above grade level of gasoline fuel dispensing pumps are designated as _____ locations.

A. Class I, Division 1
B. Class I, Division 2
C. Class II, Division 1
D. Class II, Division 2

34. The service equipment for floating docks or marinas shall be located _____ the floating structure.

   I. adjacent to
   II. on or in

A. I only
B. II only
C. either I or II
D. neither I nor II

35. The disconnecting means shall be _____ of the electric sign or outline lighting that it controls.

   I. within sight or capable of being locked in the open position
   II. visible and within 50 feet

A. I only
B. II only
C. either I or II
D. both I and II

36. A run of flexible metal conduit (FMC) is permitted for use as an equipment grounding conductor, if the conductors contained within the FMC are protected by an overcurrent device rated _____.

A. 20 amperes or more
B. 20 amperes or less
C. 30 amperes or more
D. 30 amperes or less

37. Marinas and boatyards shall be provided with an insulated copper equipment grounding conductor NOT smaller than size _____.

A. 12 AWG
B. 10 AWG
C. 8 AWG
D. 6 AWG

38. Receptacles rated _____ or less directly connected to aluminum conductors shall be marked CO/ALR.

A. 20 amperes
B. 25 amperes
C. 30 amperes
D. 50 amperes

39. Direct-buried conductors and cables emerging from the ground and extending up a pole shall be protected to a point above finished grade of at LEAST _____.

A. 10 feet
B. 6 feet
C. 8 feet
D. 12 feet

40. Disregarding exceptions, where raceways containing ungrounded conductors of size _____ or larger enter a junction box, panelboard or switchboard, the conductors shall be protected by a fitting providing a smoothly rounded insulating surface.

A. 10 AWG
B. 8 AWG
C. 6 AWG
D. 4 AWG

41. Where a single equipment grounding conductor is run with multiple circuits in the same raceway, it shall be _____.

A. omitted
B. sized for the largest conductor in the raceway
C. sized for the largest overcurrent device protecting conductors in the raceway
D. sized for the smallest overcurrent device protecting conductors in the raceway

42. When sizing time-delay Class CC fuses for motor branch-circuit, short-circuit and ground-fault protection, they are to be sized at the same value as _____.

A. inverse time circuit breakers
B. non-time delay fuses
C. instantaneous trip circuit breakers
D. adjustable trip circuit breakers

43. Fixed outdoor electric deicing and snow-melting equipment shall be considered as a _____ load.

A. intermittent
B. coincidental
C. noncontinuous
D. continuous

44. When using liquidtight flexible metal conduit (LFMC) to enclose service entrance conductors, and the equipment bonding jumper is routed with the LFMC, the conduit may have a MAXIMUM length of _____.

A. 24 inches
B. 6 feet
C. 10 feet
D. 48 inches

45. Which of the following electrical equipment, if any, is permitted to be connected to the supply side of a service disconnecting means?

   I. instrument transformers
   II. Type 2 surge-protective devices

A. I only
B. II only
C. neither I nor II
D. both I and II

46. A single, GFCI protected, twist-lock, grounding type receptacle that provides power to a pool recirculating pump motor, shall be permitted NOT less than _____ from the inside wall of the pool.

A. 6 feet
B. 5 feet
C. 8 feet
D. 10 feet

47. Where a 20 ampere rated branch-circuit serves two (2) or more receptacles, the receptacles shall be rated at _____.

   I. 20 amperes
   II. 15 amperes

A. I only
B. II only
C. either I or II
D. neither I nor II

48. The NEC® permits a MAXIMUM number of _____ size 12 AWG conductors to be installed in a 3 in. x 2 in. x 1½ in. deep device box.

A. six
B. five
C. four
D. three

49. When using the general method of calculation, the demand factor to be applied on the ungrounded service-entrance conductors for six (6) residential electric clothes dryers is _____.

A. 75 percent
B. 85 percent
C. 65 percent
D. 70 percent

50. Which one of the following rooms in a dwelling is NOT required to have a wall switch controlled lighting outlet?

A. bathroom
B. bedroom
C. kitchen
D. attached garage

END OF UNIT NINETEEN

NOTES

UNIT TWENTY
FINAL EXAM # 3

RANDOM QUESTIONS THROUGHOUT THE NEC®.

This is an "OPEN BOOK" practice electricians' exam. A 2011 edition of the NATIONAL ELECTRICAL CODE is the only reference that should be used on this exam. This practice exam is typical of questions encountered on all electricians' exams. Select the best answer from the choices given then review your answers with the answer key at the back of this book.

ALLOTED TIME: 2½ hours

1. When a galvanized eye-bolt is used as the point of attachment of a service drop to a building where the voltage is 120 volts to ground, the eye-bolt shall be installed NOT less than _____ above finished grade.

A. 8 feet
B. 10 feet
C. 12 feet
D. 15 feet

2. What is the purpose of an equipment grounding conductor?

A. To reduce voltage drop.
B. To limit galvanic corrosion.
C. To reduce electrolysis.
D. To establish an effective ground-fault path and facilitate the operation of the overcurrent protective device.

3. When calculating services and feeders for commercial occupancies such as office buildings and retail stores, before demand factors are taken into consideration, all 15- and 20-ampere, 125-volt duplex receptacles are to be calculated at a value of _____ each.

A. 100 VA
B. 125 VA
C. 150 VA
D. 180 VA

4. When installing intermediate metal conduit (IMC) vertically from industrial machinery, provided the conduit is made up with threaded couplings, the distance between supports shall NOT exceed _____ .

A. 8 feet
B. 10 feet
C. 14 feet
D. 20 feet

5. Drywall or plasterboard surfaces that are damaged around boxes having a flush-type cover or faceplate shall be repaired so there will be no gaps greater than _____ at the edge of the box.

A. 1/8 in.
B. 1/4 in.
C. 3/8 in.
D. 1/2 in.

6. Type NM cable is NOT permitted for use _____.

A. in wet locations
B. in Type V construction
C. for exposed work in dry locations
D. in any of the above listed conditions or locations

7. For a small hospital, the essential electrical system shall consist of _____.

A. equipment system, transfer branch and emergency branch
B. life safety branch, critical branch and equipment system
C. emergency system, generating system and normal power system
D. normal power system, emergency system and alternate power system

8. The applied voltage for Class 1 remote-control and signaling circuits shall NOT exceed _____.

A. 24 volts
B. 30 volts
C. 150 volts
D. 600 volts

9. In regard to solar photovoltaic systems for dwellings, non lead-acid storage batteries shall have the cells connected so as to operate at LESS than _____ nominal.

A. 12 volts
B. 24 volts
C. 50 volts
D. 48 volts

10. Each grounding electrode plate shall expose NOT less than _____ of surface area to the exterior soil

A. 1 cu. ft.
B. 1½ sq. ft.
C. 2 sq. ft.
D. 3 sq. ft.

11. Where an equipment room houses electrical equipment, the personnel doors intended for entrance and egress from the working space, shall open in the direction of egress when the _____.

A. electrical equipment in the room has a rating of 800 amperes
B. electrical equipment in the room has a rating of 1000 amperes
C. electrical equipment in the room has a rating of 1400 amperes
D. equipment room is also used for storage

12. A fused disconnecting means for a motor rated 600 volts or less, shall have an ampere rating of at LEAST _____ of the full-load current rating of the motor.

A. 100 percent
B. 115 percent
C. 125 percent
D. 135 percent

13. Cabinets containing overcurrent protection devices shall NOT be located _____.

A. over uneven surfaces
B. over steps of a stairway
C. over a stairway landing
D. under a mezzanine

14. Which of the following listed is NOT permitted for use as a grounding electrode?

A. metal underground water pipe
B. ground rod 8 feet in length
C. metal underground gas pipe
D. concrete-encased building steel

15. As defined in the NEC®, a controller is any switch or device that is normally used to _____.

A. disconnect or start a motor by any means
B. control a motor by making and breaking the overload circuit current
C. stop and start a motor by making and breaking the motor control circuit current
D. start and stop a motor by making and breaking the motor circuit current

16. Where a fuse or inverse time circuit breaker responsive to motor current is used for overload protection for a hermetic motor-compressor, this device shall be rated at NOT more than _____ of the motor-compressor rated-load current.

A. 175 percent
B. 150 percent
C. 125 percent
D. 115 percent

17. In regard to solar photovoltaic systems, in event of a ground-fault, the inverter or charge controller fed by the faulted circuit shall _____.

A. sound an alarm
B. sound an alarm and energize a strobe type luminaire
C. automatically cease to supply power to output circuits
D. not automatically cease to supply power to output circuits

18. Where conductors of size 4 AWG or larger are installed in conduits entering a junction box and straight pulls of the conductors are to be made, the length of the box shall NOT be less than _____ times the trade size of the largest raceway.

A. six
B. eight
C. ten
D. twelve

19. Where a building or structure is supplied with a 3-phase, 4-wire, 480Y/277 volt service, each disconnecting means rated at LEAST _____ or more shall be provided with ground-fault protection.

A. 1000 amperes
B. 1200 amperes
C. 2000 amperes
D. 800 amperes

20. When two motors, one smaller than the other, are supplied from a common feeder and are interlocked so that only one of them can run at one time, the calculation of the ampacity of the feeder is to be based on _____.

A. the total FLC of the two motors
B. 125% of the FLC of the larger of the two
C. the sum of the FLC of the two, plus 25% of the FLC of the larger motor
D. 125% of the total FLC

21. The MINIMUM size copper equipment grounding conductor required to electrical equipment served by a 40 ampere rated branch-circuit is _____.

A. 8 AWG
B. 10 AWG
C. 12 AWG
D. 14 AWG

22. In industrial establishments, where sizes 1/0 AWG through 4/0 AWG single conductor cables are installed in a ladder type cable tray, the MAXIMUM allowable rung spacing for the ladder cable tray shall be _____.

A. 15 inches
B. 12 inches
C. 9 inches
D. 6 inches

23. Ceiling (paddle) fans weighing MORE than _____ shall be supported independently of the outlet box.

A. 30 lbs.
B. 25 lbs.
C. 50 lbs.
D. 70 lbs.

24. Where a crane is used in an area where easily ignitible fibers or flyings are present, this area is considered to be a _____ location.

A. Class I
B. Class II
C. Class III
D. Class IV

25. When circuit conductors connecting one or more units of information technology equipment to a source of supply, the conductors shall have an ampacity of NOT less that what percent of the total connected load?

A. 125 percent
B. 115 percent
C. 300 percent
D. 80 percent

26. Where conductors are installed in conduits exposed to direct sunlight 4 inches above a rooftop, a temperature adder of _____ shall be added to the outdoor temperature to determine the applicable ambient temperature for application of the correction factors in Table 310.15(B)(2)(a) of the NEC®.

A. 60° F
B. 40° F
C. 30° F
D. 25° F

27. The ultimate trip current of a thermally protected 2 hp, single-phase, 240 volt motor shall NOT exceed _____ of the full-load running current of the motor.

A. 115 percent
B. 125 percent
C. 140 percent
D. 156 percent

28. Where a central vacuum assembly is located in a storage closet adjacent to the laundry room of a dwelling, accessible non-current-carrying metal parts of the assembly likely to become energized shall be _____.

A. connected to an equipment grounding conductor
B. GFCI protected
C. insulated
D. isolated

29. In general, the disconnecting means for an air-conditioning unit _____.

A. shall not be located anywhere on the A/C unit
B. shall be located adjacent to the A/C unit
C. shall not be located on panels of the A/C unit that are designed to allow to access the unit
D. is permitted to be located on the access panels of the A/C unit, where the top of the disconnect is not within 12 inches of the top of the A/C unit

30. Low-voltage lighting systems operating at 30 volts or less are to be rated NO more than _____.

A. 30 amperes
B. 25 amperes
C. 20 amperes
D. 15 amperes

31. The NEC® states heavy-duty lighting track is lighting track identified for use _____.

A. exceeding 20 amperes
B. for more than 30 amperes
C. for less than 30 amperes
D. in commercial applications only

32. Where conductors are ran in parallel in separate raceways, each parallel equipment grounding conductor shall be sized in accordance with _____ of the NEC®.

A. Section 310.4
B. Tbl. 310.15(B)(16)
C. Tbl. 250.122
D. Tbl. 250.66

33. Disregarding exceptions, each patient bed location in critical care areas of hospitals shall be supplied by _____.

I. one or more branch-circuits from the emergency system
II. one or more branch-circuits from the normal system

A. I only
B. II only
C. either I or II
D. both I and II

34. Where electrical metallic tubing (EMT) is installed under metal-corrugated sheet roof decking, a clearance of at LEAST _____ must be maintained between the top of the tubing and the surface of the roof decking.

A. 1¼ in.
B. 1½ in.
C. 1 in.
D. 2 in.

35. The MINIMUM permitted height of a ceiling-suspended luminaire installed above the top of a bathtub rim or shower stall threshold is _____.

A. 7 ft. 6 in.
B. 8 ft.
C. 10 ft.
D. 12 ft.

36. What is the MAXIMUM number of times a grounding electrode conductor is permitted to be spliced by the use of listed split-bolt connectors?

A. one
B. two
C. three
D. none

37. In regard to an irrigation pond, the on land service equipment for floating structures and submerisible electrical equipment shall be located NO closer than _____ horizontally from the shoreline.

A. 5 feet
B. 10 feet
C. 15 feet
D. 20 feet

38. A bonding jumper NOT smaller than _____ shall be connected between the communications grounding electrode and power grounding electrode system at the building where separate electrodes are used.

A. 10 AWG
B. 8 AWG
C. 6 AWG
D. 12 AWG

39. In general, 4 in. wide underfloor raceways shall have a covering of wood or concrete of NOT less than _____ above the raceway.

A. ½ in.
B. ¾ in.
C. 1 in.
D. 1¼ in.

40. Metal conduit installed in indoor wet locations must have a MINIMUM airspace clearance of _____ between the conduit and the wall or supporting surface.

A. 1/8 in.
B. 1/4 in.
C. 1/2 in.
D. 3/8 in.

41. What is the MINIMUM size 75° C copper service-entrance conductors required for a 200 ampere rated commercial service?

A. 4/0 THW
B. 2/0 THW
C. 3/0 THHN
D. 3/0 THW

42. For motors used in a continuous duty application, the motor nameplate current rating is to be used to determine the correct size of the _____.

A. disconnecting means
B. motor circuit conductors
C. short-circuit protection
D. motor overload protection

43. A circuit disconnect shall disconnect all associated supply conductors, including the grounded neutral conductor for _____.

A. gasoline fuel dispensers
B. irrigation machines
C. GFCI protected circuits
D. hot tubs

44. In compliance with the NEC®, flexible metallic tubing (FMT) shall NOT be used in lengths over _____.

A. 10 feet
B. 8 feet
C. 6 feet
D. 5 feet

45. In kitchens of dwelling units, receptacle outlets provided for countertop surfaces shall be installed so there is a MAXIMUM distance of _____, measured horizontally, between the receptacles.

A. 12 inches
B. 24 inches
C. 6 feet
D. 4 feet

46. Overload relays and other devices for motor overload protection that are NOT capable of opening short-circuits or ground-faults shall be protected by a motor short-circuit protector or by _____.

A. an instantaneous trip circuit breaker only
B. fuses of circuit breakers
C. Class CC fuses only
D. a ground-fault circuit interrupter

47. Where the outer sheath of Type MI cable is made of steel _____.

A. a separate equipment grounding conductor shall be provided
B. it shall provide an adequate path to serve as an equipment grounding conductor
C. the grounding and grounded conductors shall be bonded together
D. it shall not be more than 6 feet in length

48. Where exposed NM cable passes through a floor, the cable shall be protected from physical damage by an approved means extending at LEAST _____ above the floor.

A. 4 inches
B. 6 inches
C. 8 inches
D. 10 inches

49. Where a dwelling unit is provided with a deck or porch that is accessible from inside the dwelling, at least one (1) 125-volt, 15- or 20-ampere receptacle outlet is required to be installed within the perimeter of the deck or porch. The receptacle shall NOT be located more than _____ above the deck or porch surface.

A. 6 feet
B. 6 1/2 feet
C. 5 feet
D. 18 inches

50. The classification of hazardous areas and zones is determined by _____.

A. engineers
B. licensed electricians
C. qualified persons
D. the local authority having jurisdiction

END OF UNIT TWENTY
****

Answer Keys
&
NEC® References

ANSWER KEY UNIT ONE

1. A 90.1(B)
2. C 90.2(A)(1)
3. C 90.4
4. D 90.6
5. D 90.2(C)
6. D 90.5(A)
7. A Art. 100
8. A Art. 100
9. B Art. 100
10. D Art. 100
11. C Art. 100
12. B Art. 100
13. A Art. 100
14. A Art. 100
15. A Art. 100
16. D Art. 100
17. A Art. 100
18. B Art. 100
19. D Art. 100
20. C Art. 100
21. C Art. 100
22. D Art. 100
23. C 110.5
24. D 110.12
25. C 110.6
26. A 110.14

27. C 110.7
       90.1(B)
28. A 110.14(A)
29. C Tbl. 110.26(A)(1)
30. C 110.26(C)(2)
31. A 110.26(A)(3)
32. B 110.12(A)
33. B 110.31
34. B 110.27(A)(4)
35. A Tbl. 110.28
36. B 110.26(A)(2)
37. B Tbl. 110.26(A)(1)
38. A 110.26(F)
39. A 110.74
40. C 110.75(A)
41. D 110.75(D)
42. B 110.77
43. D 110.3(A)(1),(2) &(3)
44. A 110.16
45. A 110.26(C)(3)
46. B 200.6(A)
47. A 200.10(B)(1)
48. A 200.6(B)(3)
49. D 200.6(E)
50. B 200.11

ANSWER KEY UNIT TWO

1. D 210.6(A)(1)
2. B 210.8(A)(6)
3. B 210.5(C)(1)
4. B 210.19(A)(3)
5. D 210.19(A)(1)
6. A 210.52(H)
7. A 210.12(A), IN #1
8. D 210.21(B)(1)
9. B 210.23(B)
10. D 210.52(C)(1)
11. B Tbl. 210.21(B)(2)
12. A 210.8(B)(1)
13. A 210.11(C)(3)
14. C 210.4(A)
15. B 210.8(A)(6)
16. B 210.52(C)(5)
17. D 210.8(A)(3), Ex.
18. C Tbl. 210.21(B)(3)
19. D 210.12(A)
20. B 210.8(A)(2)
21. C 210.8(A)(1),(2),&(3)
22. A 210.23(A)(1)
23. C 210.52(A)(1)
24. A 210.52(A)(2)(1)
25. B 210.52(A)(3)

26. D 210.52(C)(1)
27. B 210.52(C)(2)
28. B 210.52(D)
29. C 210.63
30. C 210.50(C)
31. A 210.11(C)(1),(2),&(3)
32. A 210.8(A)(3)
33. B 210.62
34. C 210.52(4)
35. B 210.60(B)
36. C 210.52(I)
37. A 210.52(B)(1), Ex. 2
38. D 210.52(G)(1)
39. D 210.70 (A)(2)(a) & (b)
40. D 210.70(A)(3)
41. C 210.52(E)(1)
42. D 210.11(C)(1)
43. C 210.70(A)(2)(C)
44. D 210.70(A)(1), Ex. 2
45. B Tbl. 210.21(B)(2)
46. A 210.8(B)(2)
47. D 210.18
       210.12(A)
48. C 210.52(G)(1)
       210.70(A)(3)
49. B 210.8(A)(2)
50. D 210.63, Ex.

ANSWER KEY UNIT THREE

1. B 215.4(A)
2. C 215.4(B)
3. A 215.3
4. D 215.10
5. D 220.54
6. C Tbl. 220.12
7. D 220.61(B)
8. B 220.14(K)(2)
9. A 220.(52)(B)
10. B Tbl. 220.55, Col. C
11. A 220.14(J)
12. C 220.14(I)
13. A 220.53
14. D 220.18(B)
15. C Tbl. 220.103
16. D 225.18(4)
17. A 225.19(B)
18. B 225.6(A)(1)
19. B 225.18(2)
20. A. 225.39(A)
21. A 230.2
22. B 230.26
23. C 230.43(13)
24. B 230.79(C)
25. A 230.7, Ex.1

26. C 230.2(B)(2) & 230.2(C)(1)
27. C 230.71(B)
28. A 230.31(B)
29. C 230.28
30. D 230.31(B), Ex.
31. A 230.6(1)
32. D 230.72(C), Ex.
33. D 230.95
34. A 230.205(A)
35. B 230.51(A)
36. B 230.43(5)
37. B 230.9(A)
38. A 230.95(A)
39. D 230.42(B)
40. D 230.71(A)
41. A 240.6(A)
42. D 240.4(C) & 240.6(A)
43. C 240.4(B) & 240.6(A)
44. C 240.24(D)&(E)
45. D 240.21(B)(1)(1)a.
46. D 240.50(C)
47. D 240.6(A)
48. B 240.21(B)(4)&(4)(9)
49. A 240.51(B)
50. C 240.83(D)

ANSWER KEY UNIT FOUR

1. A   250.24(C)(1)
2. C   250.52(A)(1)
3. B   250.68(A), Ex.1
4. C   250.53(G)
5. A   250.8(A)
6. A   250.52(B)(1)
       250.52(A)(1),(2)&(5)
7. A   250.64(E)
8. C   250.52(A)(5)(b)
9. A   250.64(A)
10. B   Tbl. 250.122
11. C   250.52(A)(5)(a)
12. C   250.122(B)
13. D   250.4(A)(4) & (5)
14. D   250.24(A)(1)
15. B   250.94
16. C   250.52(A)(7)
17. B   250.86,Ex.2
18. B   Tbl. 250.66
19. D   250.122(C) & Tbl. 250.122
20. C   250.178
21. A   250.66(A)
22. B   Tbl. 250.66
23. D   250.24(A)(5)
24. A   250.52(A)(3)(2)
25. C   250.53(B)

26. B   250.52(A)(4)
27. C   250.52(B)(1) & 250.104(B)
28. A   250.53(D)(2)
29. D   250.52(A)(2)(1)
30. A   250.68(A) & Ex.
31. D   250.64(B)
32. B   250.122(F)
33. D   250.24(C)
34. A   250.97(2)
35. A   250.118(2),(3)&(4)
36. A   250.119
37. C   250.102(E)(2)
38. C   250.106
39. C   250.52(A)(5)
40. A   Tbl. 250.66
41. A   250.52(B)(2)
42. B   250.102(C) & Tbl. 250.66
43. B   250.118(5)b.
44. D   250.53(G)
45. D   250.148(C)
46. B   250.66(A)
47. A   250.58
48. C   250.30(A)(4)(1) & (2)
49. C   250.53(A)(2), Ex.
50. D   250.104(A)(1)

ANSWER KEY UNIT FIVE

1. D 300.16(A)
2. B Tbl. 300.5, Col. 2
3. B Tbl. 300.5, Col. 4
4. A Tbl. 300.5, Col. 1-5
5. D 300.22(A)
6. B 300.21
7. B 300.5(H)
8. C 300.4(A)(1)
9. B 300.6(D)
10. A 300.5(D)(1)
11. A 300.20(A)
12. A 300.13(A)
13. D 300.5(J) & IN
14. D 300.13(B)
15. C Tbl. 300.19(A)
16. A 300.4(A)(2) 310.15(B)(16)
17. B 300.20(A)
18. D 300.14
19. B Tbl. 300.50
20. C 300.5(D)(3)
21. C 300.9
22. D 300.4(E)
23. A 300.3(C)(1)
24. D 300.4(G)
25. B 300.40

26. D Tbl. 300.19(A)
27. D 300.3(C)(2)(c)
28. D 300.22(C)(1)
29. B 310.15(B)(5)(a) & (c)
30. C 310.10(H)(2),(1) & (2)
31. D Tbl. 310.104(A)
32. C Tbl. 310.15(B)(7)
33. D 310.106(C)
34. B 310.10(A),(B), & (C)
35. B Tbl. 310.15(B)(3)(a)
36. A Tbl. 310.15(B)(2)(a)
37. D 310.15(B)(3)(2)
38. C Tbl. 310.104(A)
39. D Tbl. 310.15(B)(17)
40. D Tbl. 310.104(A)
41. C Tbl. 310.104(A) & Tbl
42. B 310.15(A)(3)
43. A 310.10(H)
44. B Tbl. 310.15(B)(3)(c)
45. D 310.10(H)(5)
46. C 310.15(B)(3)
47. D Tbl. 310.104(A)
48. B Tbl. 310.15(B)(7)
49. D Tbl. 310.15(B)(16)
50. A 310.120(B)(1)

ANSWER KEY UNIT SIX

1. A 314.20
2. B 314.16(B)(3)
3. B 314.16(B)(2)
4. C 314.16(B)(4)
5. A 314.23(B)(1)
6. D 314.28(A)(1)
7. D 314.17(C), Ex
8. D 314.23(B)(2)
9. C 314.24(A)
10. B 314.23(F)
11. B 314.24(B)(4)
12. C Tbl. 314.16(B)
13. D Tbl. 314.16(A)
14. A 314.21
15. C 314.27(A)(2)
16. D 314.16(B)(4)
17. A 314.41
18. D 314.71(A)
19. D 314.30(D)
20. A 314.27(C)
21. C 320.100
22. A 320.80(A)
23. D 320.30(B)
24. B 320.24
25. C 320.30(D)(3)

26. A 320.10(1)
        320.12(1)&(2)
27. A 324.10(B)(2)
28. D 324.1 & 324.10(D)
29. C 324.100
30. A 324.12(4)
31. B 324.41
32. D 324.10(B)(1)
33. C 326.10 & 12
34. D 326.104
35. B 326.2
36. A Tbl. 326.80
37. D 328.10
38. D 328.10(3)-(5)
39. C 328.80
40. D 330.104
41. C 330.24(A)(2)
42. D 330.30(D)(2)
43. B 330.24(B)
44. D 330.10(A)(6),(7) &(8)
        330.12(2)b.
45. A 330.30(B)
46. A 332.30
47. A 332.108
48. C 332.24
49. A 332.10(1),(5),(7)&(8)
50. B 332.104

ANSWER KEY UNIT SEVEN

1. B 334.10(4) & 334.12(A)(3)
2. C 334.112 & IN
3. B 334.104
4. D 334.15(C)
5. B 334.15(B)
6. B 334.30
7. D 334.80
8. C 334.116(B)
9. A 334.12(B)(4)
10. A 338.10(B)(1)
11. A 338.24
12. C 338.12(B)(1) & 338.100
13. A 340.80
14. C 340.104
15. D 340.10(2) & 300.3(B)
16. D 340.10(4) & 340.12(1),(4) & (5)
17. B 340.108
18. C 342.28
19. D 342.30(B)(1)
20. B 342.20(B)
21. D 342.42(A)
22. C 342.30(B)(3)
23. A 344.24 & Tbl. 2, Chpt. 9
24. D Tbl. 344.30(B)(2)
25. D 344.20(B)

26. C 344.14 & 344.60
27. B 344.30(A)
28. C 344.42(A) & 314.15
29. A 348.30(A) & (B)
30. B 348.20(A)(2)(c)
31. D 348.20(B)
32. D 348.12(1)
33. C Tbl. 348.22
34. A 348.42
35. D 350.26
36. C 350.60
37. B 350.20(A)
38. A 350.30(A)
39. D 352.12(B) & (C)
40. D Tbl. 352.30
41. D 352.30(A)
42. A 352.26
43. A 352.12(D)
44. B Tbl. 352.44
45. D 352.20(B)
46. D 356.20(A)(1) & (2)
47. B 356.30(3)
48. C 356.10(3) & (7) 356.12(1)
49. D 356.20(B)
50. C 356.24 & Tbl. 2, Chpt. 9

ANSWER KEY UNIT EIGHT

1. A 358.42
2. B 358.28(B), Ex. & 358.100
3. C 358.20(B)
4. C 358.24
5. B 358.30(A)
6. D 358.30(B)
7. D 360.20(B)
8. A 360.12(6)
9. D 362.12(5)
10. B 362.20(B)
11. C 362.12(3)
12. C 362.10(2), Ex.
13. A 366.30(B)
14. C 366.22(A)
    Tbl. 310.15(B)(3)(a)
15. D 366.56(A)
16. D 366.12(2)
17. A 366.100(E)
18. D 366.22(A)
19. B 368.30
20. C 368.17(B), Ex.
21. D 368.58 & 368.60
22. D 368.12(A),(B) & (D)
23. B 370.4(C)
24. D 370.4(A)
25. C 370.6(A)

26. C 376.22(B)
27. C 376.30(B)
28. B 376.22(A)
29. D 376.56(A)
30. A 378.30(A)
31. B 378.44
32. D 378.23(B) & 314.28(A)(2)
33. A 378.10(2) & 378.12(2)
34. C 378.22
35. A 382.120(A)
36. D 382.15(A)
37. C 382.30(A)
38. B 382.12(2)
39. B 384.10(7) & 384.12(1)
40. D 384.30(B)
41. B 384.2 & 384.100(A)
42. D 386.22(2)
43. A 386.10(1) & (4)
44. C 386.60
45. B 386.12(2)
46. C 388.12(3)
47. B 388.56
48. D 388.30
49. C 388.70
50. B 388.56

ANSWER KEY UNIT NINE

1. B 390.4(A)
2. D 390.8
3. C 392.10(B)(1)(c)
4. D 392.10(B)(1)(a)
5. C Tbl. 392.60(A), Note b
6. D 392.60(B)(1) & (3)
7. A 392.12
8. A 392.22(A)(3)(a)
9. B 392.20(B)(1)
10. B 392.80(A)(2)(c)
    Tbl. 310.15(B)(17)
11. A 392.56
12. B Tbl. 392.22(A)
13. D 394.30(A)(1)&(2)
14. A 394.56
15. C 394.19(C) & 398.19
16. C 394.17
17. D Tbl. 396.10(A)
18. B 396.2
19. D 396.30(A)
20. A 396.10(B)
21. D 398.10
22. D 398.15(C)
23. A 398.30(D)
24. D Tbl. 400.4
25. D Tbl. 400.5(A)(1), Col. 2

26. B 400.7(A)(2),(3)&(8)
    400.8(2)
27. C 400.11
28. A 400.31(A)
29. B 400.5(A)
30. C 400.22(C)
31. C 402.6
32. B Tbl. 402.5
33. A Tbl. 402.3
34. D Tbl. 402.3
35. D Tbl. 402.3
36. D 404.8(A)
37. B 404.13(A)
38. B 404.8(B)
39. A 404.2(A)
40. C 404.14(A)(3)
41. C 404.14(C)
42. B 404.14(E)
43. D 406.9(C)
44. A 406.10(B)(1)
45. C 406.3(C)
46. B 406.5(E)
47. A 406.3(D)
48. A 406.9(B)(1)
49. C 406.9(A) & (B)
50. D 406.4(D)(2)(c)

ANSWER KEY UNIT TEN

1. B 408.3(E)
2. A 408.36(A)
3. B 408.36, Ex. 3
4. C 408.5
5. A 408.3(E)
6. A Tbl. 408.5
7. B 408.3(C)
8. D 408.19
9. B 408.37
      312.2
10. A 408.18(B)
       110.26(A)(3)
11. C 408.36, Ex. 2
12. C 408.40
13. D 408.3(E), IN
       110.15
14. B 408.18(A)
15. A 408.18(B)
       Tbl. 110.26(A)(1)
16. B 410.10(D)
17. B 410.68
18. D 410.11
19. C 410.16(C)(1)
20. A 410.117(C)
21. B 410.116(A)(1)
22. C 410.62(C)(1)(2)a.
23. B 410.6
24. D 410.5, Ex.
25. D 410.10(D)

26. C 410.30(A)
27. A 410.54(C)
28. D 410.136(B)
29. A 410.30(B)(1)
30. B 410.116(B)
31. C 422.11(C)
32. D 442.13
       422.10(A)
33. C 422.16(B)(1)(2)
34. D 422.16(B)(2)(2)
35. D 422.11(E)(3)
36. B 422.51
37. A 422.31(A)
38. A 422.11(E)(1)
39. D 422.15(C)
40. C 424.3(A)
41. D 424.3(B)
       210.19(A)(1)
42. D 424.22(B)
43. C 424.20(A)(3)
44. D 424.22(B)
45. B 424.35(2)
46. A 424.36
47. A 424.38(A)
48. C 424.44(A)
49. C 426.4
       210.19(A)(1)
50. D 426.20(A)

ANSWER KEY UNIT ELEVEN

1. C 430.6(A)(2)
2. A 430.42(C)
3. B 430.22
4. D 430.52(C)(1) & Tbl. 430.52
5. C 430.110(A)
6. C 430.7(A)(1),(2) & (5)
7. A 430.75(B)
8. B 430.82(C)(2)
9. B 430.109(C)(2)
10. A 430.232
11. D 430.81(B)
12. B 430.33
13. C 430.6(B)
14. C 430.52(C)(1),Ex.2(c)
15. C Tbl. 430.250
16. A 430.6(A)(2) & 430.32(C)
17. D 430.44 & 430.225(A),Ex.
18. B 430.6(A)(1) & 430.52(C)(1) Tbl. 430.52
19. B 430.24,Ex.3
20. D 430.75(A)
21. D 430.84,Ex.
22. D 430.24(1)
23. B 430.102(B)(2), Ex.
24. B 430.32(A)(1)
25. A 430.22(E)
26. B 430.40
27. D 440.52(A)(1)
28. C 440.62(B)
29. A 440.52(A)(3)
30. D 440.14
31. C 440.64
32. B 440.55(B)
33. D 440.22(A),Ex.
34. D 445.11
35. B 445.13
36. D 445.14
37. A 450.43(B)
38. C 450.13(B)
39. B 450.11
40. A 450.21(B)
41. D 450.4(A)
42. A Tbl. 450.3(B)
43. D 455.9
44. C 455.6(A)(1)
45. B 455.8
46. B 460.2(A)
47. C 460.8(A)
48. A 460.9
49. D 480.9(A)
50. C 480.10(A)

ANSWER KEY UNIT TWELVE

1. C 500.6(B)(1)
2. A 500.5(B)(1), IN #2(5)
3. C 500.5(C)(1)(1)
4. D 500.5(B)(1)(1)
5. C 500.5(D)
6. B 500.5(B)(1), IN #1(2)
7. A 500.7(A)
8. D 500.7(C) & 502.10(B)(4)
9. B 500.8(E)(1)
10. A 500.8(E)(2)
11. B 501.15(A)(1)
12. C 501.15(A)(4)
13. C 501.15(C)(3)
14. B 501.10(B)(2)(2)
15. B 501.30(A)
16. A 501.15(C)(6)
17. D 501.30(B), Ex.(1) & (2)
18. B 501.100(A)(1)
19. A 502.30(A)
20. C 502.10(A)(1)(2)
21. C 502.15(2)
22. A 502.115(B)
23. B 502.10(A)(1)(4)
24. C 502.100(A)(1)
25. A 502.130(B)(4)

26. B 503.130(B)
27. C 503.10(A)(1)(1)
28. D 503.115
29. A 511.3
30. A 511.3(C)(3)(b)
31. B 511.3(C)(1)(a)
32. C 511.12
33. D 511.7(A)(1)
34. D 511.7(B)(1)(b)
35. B 511.3(C)(1)(b)
36. D 511.4(B)(2)
37. B 514.9(A)
38. A 514.11(A)
39. A 514.8, Ex. 2
40. D 514.11(B)
41. D Tbl. 514.3(B)(1)
42. D 514.11(A)
43. A Tbl. 514.3(B)(1)
44. D Tbl. 514.3(B)(1)
45. B 515.8(A)
46. B Tbl. 515.3
47. C 515.7(A)
48. D 516.4(C)(2) & (4)
49. C 516.10(A)(6)
50. B 516.3(C)(2)(b)

ANSWER KEY UNIT THIRTEEN

1. C   517.19(B)(1)
2. B   517.18(B)
3. D   517.13(B), Ex. 2
4. D   517.18(A) & (B)
5. A   517.64(A)(1)
6. C   517.33(A)(3)(g) & (8)(f)
7. C   517.14
8. A   517.2
9. B   517.42
10. D   517.33(A)(3)b. & c. & (7)
11. B   517.31
12. D   517.60(A)(1)
13. D   517.72(A)
        660.5
14. B   517.35(B)(1)
15. C   517.71(A), Ex.
16. D   517.160(A)(2)
17. D   518.2(A)
18. D   518.1 & 2(A)
19. C   518.3(B)
20. B   518.4(A)
21. B   520.41(A)
22. D   520.25(C)
23. C   520.45
24. A   520.25(A)
25. B   520.42

26. C   520.5(A)
27. A   525.5(B)
28. A   525.21(A)
29. B   525.20(B)
30. B   525.22(A)
31. B   525.11
32. C   525.10(A)
33. A   530.18(E)
34. C   530.12(A)
35. D   530.18(A)
36. D   547.2
37. D   547.5(A)
38. B   547.5(B)
39. B   547.10(B)
40. D   547.8(C)
41. B   547.9(A)(7)
42. B   550.32(C)
43. D   Tbl. 550.31
44. C   550.32(A)
45. C   550.10(I)(1)
46. B   550.10(G)
47. B   550.31(1)
48. C   550.10(D)
49. A   550.10(A)
50. A   550.32(F)

ANSWER KEY UNIT FOURTEEN

1. B 551.71
2. C 551.45(B)
3. D 551.73(A)
4. A Tbl. 551.73(A)
5. A 551.77(D)
6. D 551.71
7. B 551.78(A)
8. C 551.80(B)
9. B 552.2
10. B 552.44(B)
11. C 552.44(E)
12. B 555.15(B)
13. C 555.19(A)(4)
14. D Tbl. 555.12, Note 1
15. B 551.21(B)(2)(a)
16. A 555.17(B)
17. C 590.3(B)
18. B 590.6(B)(2)(3)d.
19. A 590.6(B) & (B)(1)
20. C 600.2 & 3(A)
21. A 600.5(B)(1)
22. B 600.5(B)(2)
23. D 600.6(A)(1) ART. 100
24. B 600.21(E)
25. B 600.6(B)

26. D 600.9(A)
27. C 600.10(D)(2)
28. A 600.5(A)
29. C 600.10(B) & (C)(2)
30. C 600.5(C)(3) 410.30(B)(1)
31. A 600.32(K)
32. C 600.5(B)(2)
33. C 620.12(A)(1)
34. A 620.61(B)(1)
35. A 620.21(A)(3)(a)
36. D 620.32
37. C 620.85
38. B 620.21(A)(1)(d)
39. B 620.37(C)
40. A 625.17
41. D 625.21
42. C 625.29(B)
43. B 626.11(A)
44. A 626.22(B)
45. C 626.24(B)(1) & (2)
46. A Tbl. 630.11(A)
47. B 630.12(A)
48. D 630.32(B)
49. B 630.42(C)
50. C 630.41

ANSWER KEY UNIT FIFTEEN

1. D   645.5(E)(2)
2. D   645.5(A)
3. A   645.15
4. B   645.10(A)
5. C   645.5(G)
6. D   645.4(5)
7. C   645.3(A)
          300.21
8. A   645.15
9. B   647.6(B)
10. B   647.1
11. C   660.4(A)
12. A   660.2
13. B   660.6(A)
14. A   660.5
15. D   660.9
16. B   665.1
17. C   665.12
18. A   665.10(A)
19. D   668.1
20. C   668.12(A)
21. A   668.20(A)
22. A   675.2
23. B   675.10(A)(3)
24. D   675.4(C)
25. C   675.11(A)

26. A   675.22(A)
27. C   680.22(A)(3)
28. A   680.58
29. B   680.24(A)(2)(b)
30. D   680.22(B)(2)(1)
31. C   680.62(E)
32. A   680.43(A)
33. D   680.23(B)(3)
34. C   680.26(B) & (B)(1)(a)
35. A   680.7(A)
36. B   680.22(C)
37. D   680.41
38. C   680.32
39. D   680.23(F)(2)
40. D   680.23(B)(2)(a)
41. C   Fig. 680.8 & Tbl. 680.8
42. C   680.23(B)(2)(b)
43. A   680.43(A)(1)
44. A   680.26(B)(7), Ex. 2
45. B   680.21(A)(1)
46. C   680.57(C)(1)
47. C   680.10 & Tbl. 680.10
48. D   680.9
49. B   680.22(B)(1)
50. A   680.42(A)(2)

ANSWER KEY UNIT SIXTEEN

1. D 682.13
2. D 682.11
3. A 682.15
4. C 682.2
5. B 682.33(C)
6. B 682.33(A)
7. C 690.7(D)
8. B 690.71(B)(1)
9. A 690.64
       705.12(D)
10. B 690.41
11. D 690.4(B)
12. B 690.8(A)(1)
13. A 690.9(D)
14. B 690.31(A)
15. C 690.31(B)
16. A 690.33(D)
17. C 690.42, IN
18. B 690.54
19. B 690.64
       705.12(D)(2)
20. C 695.14(D)
21. D 695.12(D)
22. A 695.4(B)(2)(a)
23. D 695.6(C)
24. B 695.7(B)
25. A 700.10(A)

26. D 700.12(F)
27. A 700.11(D)(1)(4)
28. C 700.12(A)
29. D 700.20
30. D 700.12(A), (B) & (D)
31. D 700.6(B) & (C)
32. C 700.12(B)(2)
33. A 700.12(B)(5)
34. B 700.5(A)
35. C 700.12(A)
36. C 701.2
37. B 701.12(A)
38. A 701.12
39. D 701.12(G)
40. D 702.5
41. C 702.2
42. B 725.41(A)
43. C 725.43
44. A 725.24
45. D 725.51(A)
46. D 725.48(B)(1)
47. C 725.136(H)
48. A 725.179(G)
49. D Fig. 725.154(G)
50. B 725.139(C)

ANSWER KEY UNIT SEVENTEEN

1. D   760.130(B)(3)
2. A   760.49(A)
3. C   760.43
4. A   760.51(A)
5. B   760.53
6. A   760.53(A)(1)
7. C   760.48(A) & (B)
8. A   760.179(H)
9. C   760.179(C)
10. C   760.53(A)(2)
11. D   760.130(B)(1)
12. D   760.41(B) & 760.121(B)
13. B   760.3(A)
         300.21
14. D   760.127
15. A   760.136(D)(1)
16. C   760.25
17. D   760.176
18. D   760.176(B)
19. D   770.133(A)
20. B   770.2
21. C   770.106(B)
22. A   800.154(A)
         Tbl. 800.154(a)
23. D   800.44(B)
24. A   800.133(A)(2)
25. A   800.53

26. B   800.26
         300.21
27. D   800.100(D)
28. C   800.44(A)(4)
29. D   800.47(A)
30. A   800.50(B)
31. A   800.90(A)
32. C   800.90(A), IN #2(2)
33. B   800.100(A)(3)
34. C   800.179
35. B   810.58(B)
36. A   Tbl. 810.16(A)
37. C   Tbl. 810.52
38. B   820.15
39. D   820.44(E)(3)
40. A   Chpt. 9, Note 4 to Tbls.
41. C   Chpt. 9, Tbl. 1
42. B   Chpt. 9, Tbl. 4
43. C   Chpt. 9, Tbl. 4
44. D   Chpt. 9, Tbl. 5
45. A   Chpt. 9, Tbl. 8
46. B   Chpt. 9, Tbl. 2
47. A   Chpt. 9, Note 9 to Tbls.
48. A   Chpt. 9, Note 9 to Tbls.
49. C   Annex C, Tbl. C.10
50. B   Annex C, Tbl. C.1

ANSWER KEY UNIT EIGHTEEN

1. C   Art. 100 Def.
2. C   Art. 100 Def.
3. B   230.6(1) & (2)
4. D   230.3
5. B   300.5(D)(3)
6. B   250.102(E)(2)
7. C   230.23(B)
8. B   300.40
9. D   250.53(G)
10. C   Tbl. 310.104(A)
11. D   702.5
12. A   310.10(H)(1)
13. C   210.52(C)(5)
14. D   404.8(A)
15. B   Tbl. 300.5
16. B   314.16(B)(2)
17. C   410.116(B)
18. C   348.20(A)(2)(c)
19. A   503.130(A)
20. B   368.30
21. B   210.60(B)
22. D   326.104
23. B   502.10(A)(4)
24. D   680.74
25. B   210.63
26. B   300.4(B)(1)

27. A   250.28(D)(1), 250.102(C) Tbl. 250.66
28. D   430.109(B)
29. B   Art. 100 Def.
30. A   424.44(G)
31. A   240.83(D)
32. C   445.12(C)
33. D   520.53(H)(2)
34. A   Tbl. 514.3(B)(1)
35. D   501.10(B)(1)(6)
36. C   455.2
37. B   250.53(B)
38. B   430.32(A)(1)
39. A   680.22(D)
40. C   314.23(B)(1)
41. C   500.6(B)(1)
42. B   410.68
43. B   517.32(H)
44. C   250.122(B)
45. D   220.12
46. B   Chpt. 9, Tbl. 1
47. D   314.16(B)(4)
48. A   300.20(A)
49. D   800.25
50. B   300.34

ANSWER KEY UNIT NINETEEN

1. C   Tbl. 344.30(B)(2)
2. A   334.24
3. B   250.52(A)(4)
4. D   Art. 100 Def.
5. A   300.14
6. A   110.26(E)(1)(a)
7. B   680.71
8. C   680.9
9. A   Note 2, to Tbl. 300.5
10. A   240.6(C)
11. B   505.8(G)
12. D   480.9(A)
13. B   230.24(B)(1)
14. A   314.20
15. C   430.83(C)(2)
16. B   210.8(A)(2)
17. D   310.106(C)
18. D   324.10(B)(1)&(2)
        324.10(D)
19. A   430.83(D)
20. B   300.22(B)
21. D   Tbl. 430.72(B)
22. C   700.1
23. B   334.104
24. C   Tbl. 300.50
25. C   240.21(C)(3)

26. C   514.11(B)
27. D   230.71(B)
28. D   250.58
29. B   450.13(B)
30. D   Art.100 Def.
31. D   210.70(A)(1), Ex. #2
32. C   540.13
33. B   Tbl. 514.3(B)(1) & Fig. 514.3
34. A   555.7
35. C   600.6(A)(1) & Art. 100 Def.
36. B   250.118(5)b.
37. A   555.15(C)
38. A   406.2(C)
39. C   300.5(D)(1)
40. D   300.4(G)
41. C   250.122(C)
42. B   Tbl. 430.52, Note 1
43. D   426.4
44. B   230.43(15)
45. D   230.82(4) & (8)
46. A   680.22(A)(1)
47. C   Tbl. 210.21(B)(3)
48. D   Tbl. 314.16(A)
49. A   Tbl. 220.54
50. B   210.70(A)(1)
        210.70(A)(2)(a)

ANSWER KEY UNIT TWENTY

1. B 230.26
2. D 250.4(A)(4) & (5)
3. D 220.14(I)
4. D 342.30(B)(3)
5. A 314.21
6. A 334.12(B)(4)
7. B Fig. 517.30, No. 2
8. D 725.41(B)
9. C 690.71(B)(1)
10. C 250.52(A)(7)
11. C 110.26(C)(3)
12. B 430.110(A)
13. B 240.24(F)
14. C 250.52(B)(1)
15. D 430.2
16. C 440.52(A)(3)
17. C 690.5(B)(2)
18. B 314.28(A)(1)
19. A 230.95
       240.13
20. B 430.24, Ex. 3
21. B Tbl. 250.122
22. C 392.10(B)(1)(a)
23. D 314.27(C)
24. C 610.3(A)(3)
25. A 645.5(A)

26. C Tbl. 310.15(B)(3)(c)
27. D 430.32(A)(2)
28. A 422.15(C)
29. C 440.14
30. B 411.2
31. A 410.153
32. C 310.10(H)(3)&(5)
       250.122(F)
33. D 517.19(A)
34. B 300.4(E)
35. B 410.10(D)
36. B 250.64(C)
37. A 682.11
38. C 800.100(D)
39. B 390.4(A)
40. B 300.6(D)
41. D Tbl. 310.15(B)(16)
42. D 430.6(A)(2)
43. A 514.11(A)
44. C 360.12(6)
45. D 210.52(C)(1)
46. B 430.40
47. A 332.108
48. B 334.15(B)
49. B 210.52(E)(3)
50. C 505.7(A)

www.ingramcontent.com/pod-product-compliance
Lightning Source LLC
Chambersburg PA
CBHW081805300426
44116CB00014B/2246